CHASING
SPIRITS

NICK GROFF

with Jeff Belanger

CHASING SPIRITS

THE BUILDING OF THE
GHOST ADVENTURES CREW

 NEW AMERICAN LIBRARY

New American Library
Published by New American Library, a division of
Penguin Group (USA) Inc., 375 Hudson Street,
New York, New York 10014, USA
Penguin Group (Canada), 90 Eglinton Avenue East, Suite 700, Toronto,
Ontario M4P 2Y3, Canada (a division of Pearson Penguin Canada Inc.)
Penguin Books Ltd., 80 Strand, London WC2R 0RL, England
Penguin Ireland, 25 St. Stephen's Green, Dublin 2,
Ireland (a division of Penguin Books Ltd.)
Penguin Group (Australia), 250 Camberwell Road, Camberwell, Victoria 3124,
Australia (a division of Pearson Australia Group Pty. Ltd.)
Penguin Books India Pvt. Ltd., 11 Community Centre, Panchsheel Park,
New Delhi - 110 017, India
Penguin Group (NZ), 67 Apollo Drive, Rosedale, Auckland 0632,
New Zealand (a division of Pearson New Zealand Ltd.)
Penguin Books (South Africa) (Pty.) Ltd., 24 Sturdee Avenue,
Rosebank, Johannesburg 2196, South Africa

Penguin Books Ltd., Registered Offices:
80 Strand, London WC2R 0RL, England

First published by New American Library,
a division of Penguin Group (USA) Inc.

First Printing, October 2012
10 9 8 7 6 5 4 3 2 1

[NAL] REGISTERED TRADEMARK—MARCA REGISTRADA

LIBRARY OF CONGRESS CATALOGING-IN-PUBLICATION DATA:

Groff, Nick.
Chasing spirits: the building of the *Ghost Adventures* crew/Nick Groff with Jeff Belanger.
    p. cm.
ISBN 978-0-451-41344-4 (pbk.)
1. Ghost adventures (Television program) 2. Parapsychology—Investigation—United States. I.
Belanger, Jeff. II. Title.
PN1992.77.G47745G76 2012
791.4572—dc23

Set in Sabon
Designed by Pauline Neuwirth

Printed in the United States of America

PUBLISHER'S NOTE
While the author has made every effort to provide accurate telephone numbers, Internet
addresses and other contact information at the time of publication, neither the publisher
nor the author assumes any responsibility for errors, or for changes that occur after
publication. Further, publisher does not have any control over and does not assume any
responsibility for author or third-party Web sites or their content.

CONTENTS

Acknowledgments   ix

Introduction   1

CHAPTER 1: Near Death   9

CHAPTER 2: Making Television   19

CHAPTER 3: Finding Virginia City   26

CHAPTER 4: The *Ghost Adventures* Crew Comes Together 41

CHAPTER 5: Investigating Virginia City   51

CHAPTER 6: Investigating the Goldfield Hotel   70

CHAPTER 7: Editing and Then Selling the Documentary   88

CHAPTER 8: Selling the Series   99

CHAPTER 9: The TV Adventure Begins   120

CONTENTS

CHAPTER 10: What's a Ghost and How Do We Find One?   147

CHAPTER 11: Possession in Savannah   160

CHAPTER 12: Favorite Cases   172

CHAPTER 13: Linda Vista Hospital: The Game Changer   199

CHAPTER 14: My Paranormal Life   217

CHAPTER 15: The Spiritual Journey   233

Paranormal Investigation Equipment   239

Appendix: Paranormal Resources   251

To my wife Veronique, our LOVE is an ADVENTURE!

—Nick Groff

ACKNOWLEDGMENTS

NICK GROFF

I would like to thank Maureen and David Groff; without them I wouldn't be here today. Thanks, Mom and Dad, for always giving me enthusiasm and courage throughout my life.

Thank you, Veronique, for always sticking by my side and guiding us throughout our journey together. I love you more than anything this world can ever offer. We are blessed to have a perfect, amazing little girl, Annabelle. I can't wait to see what the rest of our lives will hold for us.

Thank you, Grandmas Groff and Narragon. You both are amazing ladies. You have always been there for me and opened up my mind to a world that is so complex.

Thank you to my sister, Dianna, who has always had my back through good times and bad. I will never forget you buying my first tape, Compton's Most Wanted, and giving it to me on my twelfth birthday.

This dream wouldn't be a reality without the amazing people at the Travel Channel. Thank you for all of your support!

Thank you to my literary agent, Jill Marr, for believing in me and the book. Thank you to my editor, Danielle Perez, for believing in this book and for your editorial guidance. Thank you to Andy Rigrod for always having my back throughout a world of fun. It has been a blast working together! It's hard to find good people in this industry and you are truly a genuine person.

Thank you to all my friends. I raise my beer up high and drink together as one to the future. Mike Anderson, Erik Avilla, Morgan Groff, Hector Pérez Jr., Marco Bonenfant, Justin Narragon, Aaron Goodwin, Vartan and Lisa, Zak Bagans, Pete and Jim Owns, Jeff Belanger, and Danny Bedrosian.

Thank you to all my Groff and Narragon families.

THANK YOU to my amazing fans who have always been there and know who I really am. You all ROCK! Into the future we grow together.

JEFF BELANGER

Thank you, Nick, for asking me to be a part of this book. It's been a pleasure working with you on each episode of *Ghost Adventures*, and the various other opportunities that have come up along the way. I respect your honesty and work ethic and value our friendship.

Thank you to my *Ghost Adventures* family: Zak Bagans, Aaron Goodwin, Kathy DaSilva, Joe Townley, Hugh Hansen, Erik Kesten, Anthony DiDonato, Eric Paulen, and the other amazing people I've had the privilege to work with on this great show.

A big thanks to everyone at the Travel Channel who believed in *Ghost Adventures* and us!

Thank you to my wife, Megan, and daughter, Sophie, for putting up with my crazy life and for being a cheerleader when

I need it. Thank you also to Tim Weisberg, Connie Mianecki, and Edna Van Baulen.

Thank you to Jill Marr and to Danielle Perez for your help in taking this idea and turning it into a real book.

Finally, a big thanks to *Ghost Adventures* fans everywhere! Your support, ghost stories, and great attitude mean the world to me. You make all of the hard work worth it.

CHASING
SPIRITS

INTRODUCTION

Two seconds. Big, life-changing experiences don't take months or years to happen. The game changers occur in a flash of time. My life changed forever when I locked eyes with a spirit at Linda Vista Hospital in East Los Angeles during a *Ghost Adventures* lockdown. That moment—what she was wearing, the color of her eyes, her clothing, and the expression on her face—are all cut into my permanent memory like the deep scar that circles my left biceps. If I close my eyes right now, I can relive the experience just as it happened in that dark surgical suite, where the only light came from the LCD screen of my video camera.

Amid the now empty glass cabinets, the old tile walls, and the no longer used surgery lighting equipment, a woman now stood. She shouldn't have been there . . . and another second later, she was gone.

Since childhood my life has been full of paranormal experiences—yet I've always had questions. But those two seconds at Linda Vista changed me in every way. The way I deal with other people, how I think about the universe around me, and what I know about the spirit world all became clear in that moment of raw fear and shock.

My name is Nick Groff, and this is my story—how this paranormal investigator was made from the cradle to the TV screen. These are my own ghost adventures.

I'm writing this book because we can't cover all of the story in a television show. There are things the camera misses, and things the camera was never meant to see. You're about to get all of it—the successes, the fights, the challenges, and the paranormal encounters that have played a big role in making me who I am today. I want to tell you about some of my favorite cases and give you more history on the haunts that have left a mark on me.

Over the years, I've been asked a lot of questions about the paranormal, about being on a television show, and about my life. I'm going to try to answer everything I can about how I got to this point right here. I'm at a good place right now, but it can be frightening too.

I was born on April 19, 1980, in San Jose, California. Though I was born on the West Coast, I feel like more of a New England guy because my family moved to a small town in southern New Hampshire when I was one.

I grew up surrounded by woods. It was awesome. I was a hyperactive kid, and I got into a lot of trouble. Running around the woods and exploring helped me burn off some of that energy, but not all of it. There were plenty of times my adventures ended in blood.

One of my earliest memories involves my older sister, Dianna. We were jumping on the couches in the living room of our Nashua, New Hampshire, house, when all of a sudden Dianna missed and slammed her chin against the coffee table. Her chin split open and blood was everywhere. She was rushed to the hospital, where she got stitches . . . but I'll never forget the blood. The scene slowed down for me, almost the way a movie might show a tragic event in slow motion. I can still see her blood on the floor, on her hands, running down her chin and neck. I felt like a video camera capturing this scene: my sister crying, my parents frantic to comfort her and stop the bleeding. Some scenes never leave your head.

My parents, Maureen and David, tried to encourage me to be very athletic because I was always running around anyway. I was on the swim team by age four and got used to swim practice before and after school. I was a great swimmer and traveled all over the place for tournaments and meets. Looking back, I'm sure that's where I got the urge to see the world and travel to different places. When you spend a lot of time on the road, you get a sense of adventure early on. Locations have an identity and personality of their own. Some towns are depressed, others are quiet, and still others burst with energy. The people who live in such places create that energy and feed off of it at the same time.

QUESTIONS FANS ASK

What was your most frightening experience on an investigation?

At Linda Vista Hospital in Los Angeles, I came face-to-face with the spirit of a former patient. She and I locked eyes. I felt like I had a deep psychic connection with her in that moment. I will never be able to shake that one off.

After Nashua, my family moved to Salem, New Hampshire. That was an amazing place to live. My dad built a house on a cul-de-sac in an area surrounded by forest. Trees and streams and hills were everywhere around me. I was six years old and spent hours exploring the woods and building forts. Sometimes I'd be out there with my friends, but I also spent plenty of time exploring on my own. I loved the woods, loved the mystery of it, the sounds you'd hear in the distance, the strange shadows cast by the trees. An underlying sense of fear got into my blood. Every shadow was a place for something to hide or for me to explore. Like any town, the woods have a life and personality too. Looking back, I can see this was a time when the paranormal was oozing into my bloodstream.

New England is full of ghost stories and paranormal traditions. With so much history, with tales of Old World witchcraft in nearby Salem, Massachusetts, and with a population that speaks pretty openly about its haunts, how could I not become who I am today?

Sports and friends were the two biggest parts of my life as a kid. I was an adrenaline junkie even back then. I was such a strong swimmer that I broke a national record for the fifty-yard freestyle when I was ten years old. I also played soccer and basketball. I was a rowdy athlete, and that sometimes got me into trouble in school and in town. I was ultracompetitive and always wanted to win, but I loved to have a good time too.

I loved making people laugh, because that made me the center of attention . . . and it usually meant my teachers would be pissed off at me for the disruption. My parents got a lot of phone calls and had plenty of meetings with the school. My dad was a lawyer, so he had to deal with people's shit all day long, and then he'd have to come home and deal with me. Sometimes I don't know how he and my mom did it.

Don't get me wrong—I was a good student when I wanted to be. I got C's and B's. I could be smart when I was interested in something. I was lucky to have a few teachers who helped me find my way and get focused.

When I was at St. Patrick School in Pelham, New Hampshire, I had one teacher who really got through to me. Mrs. Moran saw that I was always daydreaming and making up stories. I didn't want to listen in class; I wanted to do my own thing. She helped me to develop my storytelling.

I had just seen *Cujo*, the movie about the rabid dog based on Stephen King's book. In my head I was imagining a story about a three-legged dog that followed me and my friends home. Instead of dismissing me for having crazy ideas, Mrs. Moran sat with me and helped me put them down on paper. She helped me find something I really like to do: tell stories. I think I still have that story of the three-legged dog sitting around somewhere . . . and no, you can't see it! (Just kidding . . . I will try to find it and post it on my Web site someday.) I've been a storyteller since a very young age. I still am. I always will be.

Movies were a huge influence on me too. I remember watching *E.T.* as a kid. Both the movie and the subject left a huge impact. I was blown away by the idea that UFOs could visit us, and by the incredible characters and the experiences everyone went through. Paranormal themes spoke to me even as a wide-eyed kid munching popcorn in a dark theater while watching a Steven Spielberg masterpiece.

In fact, I can't think about my childhood without also thinking about movies. I was in love with every part of the moviegoing

Has your wife ever investigated with you?

When we were in college, Veronique went with me to Virginia City and Tonopah to investigate. Now it's more just my thing. Once in a while she'll come out to a location and do a daytime walk-through with me, but she mainly leaves the ghost hunting to me now.

experience. When I sat down to watch a movie, I escaped everything. Everyday activities, anything that was frustrating about home or school was gone when the movie rolled. I would put myself in the movie—I was right there with the characters having an adventure. And when I left the theater, those adventures would continue, in the woods and in my head.

Growing up, we had only one TV with big rabbit-ear antennae, so we didn't get many channels, but of course we could rent movies. I was about six years old when I walked in on my sister watching *Alien*. I joined her, and it scared the crap out of me.

Every time I'd watch a horror movie, it would give me nightmares. I'll never forget Wes Craven's *A Nightmare on Elm Street* and the character Freddy Krueger. *Cat's Eye, Pet Sematary, Children of the Corn, It, Twilight Zone*—all these movies scared the shit out of me. I was a huge Stephen King fan back then. I loved the adrenaline rush that only fear can bring—although sometimes that made it tough for a kid to sleep. My parents would sometimes wake up in the morning and find me sleeping on the floor in their bedroom near the foot of their bed. I didn't care. I still wanted to see more horror movies. Fear made me feel alive.

I'd do anything to get my hands on more scary movies. One

time I was at the video rental store trying to rent *Dr. Giggles*. It was rated R and I was just a kid. The video clerk told me that I couldn't rent it without a parent's permission. I pointed to a woman across the store and convinced the clerk that she was my mother. When I got home, my *real* mother was pissed that I had rented the slasher film.

Maybe it was the horror movies combined with my overactive imagination, but even my room frightened me. I was scared of what might be under the bed. Some nights there was nothing and I slept fine, but on other nights I had this sense that I wasn't alone in there. It could have been just in my head, but danger lurks in funny places. By looking for ghosts and monsters, I would learn to face fear, to control it within myself.

I know children are more sensitive to the supernatural. Over time we learn to forget what we feel because adults tell us it can't be real. But what if you don't believe that? I know we say ghosts aren't real because we want to protect our children, because we want them to feel safe. Knowing what I know now, I can see I was sensitive as a kid. I've lost most of that sensitivity over the years, but not all. I don't feel I'm psychic, which can be a good thing when you're looking for ghosts. I know that if I see something it's not some psychic sense. It's real and right there. And if I can see it, my camera can see it too. I can tell the difference between my own psychic impression and what's physically in the room with me, but that skill took dozens of investigations to develop. An impression is almost like a memory, even though the event is happening in the present moment. If the spirit is manifesting in the room right now, then I'm using my regular senses to experience the entity.

My childhood was not one paranormal event after the other,

but I can look back now and see that there were events that couldn't be explained. There were connections between adventures, accidents, and life experiences that molded me into who I am today. The same could be said for all of us—we are all a product of every moment of our lives up to this point. But this is how I was drawn into the paranormal and how I launched a career on television. It wasn't a single event, but a bunch of small moments that steered me to this. Two seconds here, two seconds there, and you end up exactly where you are now.

Throughout these pages I'm going to answer some of the most common questions you've asked me on Facebook, Twitter, and in person, and I'll bare it all. We'll go behind the scenes and into my own life because I want you to see the world through my eyes. I want you to know more about the history of the locations I've investigated, and I want you to understand why I'm chasing spirits.

CHAPTER 1

NEAR DEATH

There's no question that fear sharpens your senses. When you're in a situation where your heart is racing and adrenaline is pumping, you're wide awake, you see and hear things you might not hear otherwise, and you're extra sharp. Tapping into that fear can be helpful in a paranormal investigation. Knowing fear means to know yourself. Standing in creepy, abandoned buildings frightened of what might be lurking there is one thing. Facing the real possibility of your own death is another.

My brush with death occurred when I was only eight years old. Did I mention I was a hyperactive kid? Indestructible? Looking back, I wonder if this event left me more open to the supernatural. Could coming close to my own death have brought me closer to understanding the spirit world? I'm not talking about some psychic awakening—though I know all of us have certain abilities and intuition. I mean just knowing that the spirit world is there. Recognizing the paranormal when I see it because I faced it as a kid.

Since my sister, Dianna, and I were swimmers, we spent a lot of time at the YMCA in Nashua. We had practice several times a week. My practice ended before my sister's, so my mom would take me outside and let me run around while we waited for Dianna to wrap up.

On one of these practice days, my mom sat down on a bench to read a book while I ran off to the small park behind the building. I wandered farther and farther away until I found an old tree that was begging me to climb up it. This tree stood out from the others: it was old, its branches like wrinkled arms and legs sticking out from a knotty trunk. It called to me, and soon it would punish me for my curiosity.

Part of the tree was rotten, but there were plenty of branches for me to pull myself up with. I climbed up one branch, then another. Soon I was about twelve feet off the ground, but I wasn't thinking about the height—I was thinking about the one branch that was sticking out on its own. I leaned out and grabbed the branch with my left hand, putting all of my weight on the old limb. It seemed to be holding me, so I reached out with my right hand to grab it as well. I swung my legs out from the branch I was standing on and . . .

. . . I didn't look down—not that it would have mattered had I seen the old, rusted chain-link fence directly below the branch. I wasn't thinking about falling—I was thinking about pulling myself *up* on the branch . . .

. . . *CRACK* . . . the branch snapped and I was falling.

I don't remember the fall. I don't even remember hitting the cyclone fence or the ground below. I do remember opening my eyes and seeing the tree and sky above me. I tried to stand up and look for my mom, but then everything went black and I collapsed in a heap back on the ground. Again I opened my eyes and pushed myself up. My mom was running toward me . . . something felt wet and cold on my left side. I looked at her and said, "Mom, I love you," and again it all went black and I collapsed to the ground.

What happened next was like flashes of a movie. I opened my eyes and my mother was huddled over me working on something near my body—I couldn't tell what it was. Later she told me that my left arm was ripped completely open two-thirds of the way around—the cyclone fence had sliced me up like a rusty razor. She could see my bone, my muscle was torn, and I was bleeding everywhere. I wouldn't know that until later, though at that point I did know something was very wrong.

. . . I opened my eyes and I was inside the YMCA building with a group of people standing around me. *I have to die*—that was how I felt. Like this was my time to go and that there were angels standing over me looking down. "It's going to be all right," someone said. I looked at my arm. There were T-shirts wrapped around it and everything was red, soaked with my blood.

I was in and out of consciousness, but I didn't feel any pain. I realized much later that my body was in shock—my brain had turned off all pain receptors in an effort to spare me further trauma. I opened my eyes again and was in an ambulance . . . *black* . . . I opened my eyes and was in a hospital operating room. Dianna was in there sobbing . . . *black* . . . I opened my eyes and could hear doctors working on my arm, but I still felt nothing but gentle tugs on the skin of my arm . . . *black* . . .

. . . this time I woke up in a recovery room. My mom was there. When my foggy head cleared, I heard the whole story. When I'd fallen, the top of the chain-link fence had ripped my arm open to the point where my biceps was hanging from my bone like bloody meat. Had I fallen just a quarter inch differently, the fence would have sliced through a major artery and I would not have survived. Had my mother not seen me fall and had I lain there a few extra minutes, I would have bled to death. Had my mom not been a former nurse, had she not kept a cool head and wrapped a T-shirt around my wound to stop the bleeding, I would have died. Just a few seconds had made all the difference.

I had fifty stitches on the inside of my arm and fifty stitches on the outside to pull my arm back together. You can still see the deep scar that goes almost all the way around my left bicep.

I was in a cast for a long time, and it hurt like hell after the cast was removed. My parents and coaches forced me to get back into the water and swim again as soon as the cast was off. Every stroke was painful for weeks. I know why they did that to me. I was raised to not give up, no matter how bad the setback. Had my arm been amputated, I'm sure I would have found a way to swim, to compete with only one arm.

I was only eight years old. Indestructible. It took years for this to sink in: *I could have died*. I was that close. To have your mortality tested that young changes your perspective. I couldn't have known it then, but looking back I can see it clearly: *I had a near-death experience*.

Did this horrible accident at age eight make me more careful when throwing my body into an adventure? Hell, no!

As I mentioned earlier, our house in Salem was surrounded by woods—I spent a lot of time out there having adventures as a kid. About a year after my accident, I was out in the woods one fall afternoon on a big outcropping of rocks. There was a huge tree over the rock where I had attached a rope that hung

QUESTIONS FANS ASK

How do you prepare for an investigation?

I remind myself to go in with an open mind. I'll take some deep breaths so I'm not overhyped before walking in. If you're too amped up, you'll jump at every little thing. Because I know my surroundings and the history before going in, I also feel better prepared for whatever might be inside. I can better guess at the entity's motives.

at the edge of the top of the rock. Here's how it worked: I would grab the rope and swing out over the drop-off—at least twenty feet above the ground. It was great fun—as long as the rope and tree held together, which, this day, they didn't.

I had piled up a bunch of fallen leaves at the bottom of the ledge. You know what was under those leaves? Rocks. But the fact that I'd pushed some leaves over the rocks as a cushion proves I didn't have a death wish, right? Right?!

I was out there alone on this day, swinging on my rope swing—the coolest daredevil in Salem. As I swung out I heard *CRACK, SNAP* . . . and then I was falling.

I landed on my back and my head slammed hard against the rocks under the leaves. Everything went black.

When I opened my eyes, I was dizzy, but I recognized the woods around me. I lifted myself up and stumbled around a bit. I reached my hand up to the back of my head and felt something wet. I looked at my hand and saw the blood . . . I'm thinking, *If this cut doesn't do it, Mom is going to kill me.*

I dragged myself back to our house and found my mom inside.

Off to the doctor's office we go, and three stitches on the back of my head later, I'm walking out to our car with my mother shaking her head.

Some might use the word "reckless" to describe my childhood, but to this day I say "adventurous."

At age ten, after having suffered two bloody accidents—one that almost killed me—I had my first experience with a ghost. There is definitely a connection between my near-death experience and this sighting. Something in me was open now. Now I knew what to look for and I was beginning to understand what being in the presence of a spirit feels like.

It was a school day and I had just been dropped off at home by our carpool. My mom wasn't home yet—she would usually show up five or ten minutes after me because she was working at my dad's law firm during the days while my sister and I were at school. So I used my key to get into the house.

I went in through a door on the basement level. I remember walking up the stairs from the garage and I was getting a weird feeling. I was creeped out. I knew I wasn't alone in the house. I should have been alone, but there was a presence there. It was like I was getting a premonition of something I was about to see. I was afraid and my senses were heightened by the fear.

I walked up the stairs and opened the door to the living room. I walked through the living room and into the kitchen. In our house, when you walked into the kitchen there was a dining room off to the right and a sliding glass door that looked out onto the woods in the back. I was really scared at this point and didn't know why. I had come home to an empty house many times before and thought nothing of it. But something was different today.

I tiptoed through the kitchen, leaned into the doorway, and peeked around the corner of the dining room, where I saw a figure standing there right in front of the glass door. The figure was dark, almost black. A surge of energy ran through me as I turned and sprinted through the living room, back down the stairs to the basement, and out to the side yard. I didn't stop running. Through our yard, into the woods, I jumped across a small stream and kept scrambling until I reached our neighbor's yard. I turned around. Panting from the run, I put my hands on my knees to catch my breath and I looked at our house in the distance. Something was in there. Some kind of otherworldly intruder.

At this point the experience started to sink in. I couldn't remember any features on this dark figure. I didn't see a face. It was just a tall black figure and it scared the crap out of me.

A few minutes later I saw my mom's car pull into the driveway, so I walked back to the house and went in after her. The figure, and the feeling of something being there, were now gone.

I didn't tell anyone what happened. I wasn't sure if anyone would believe me. With each hour that passed, I questioned myself. Was I just scaring myself? Was it real or not? I didn't know, but I kept checking over my shoulder for days after that experience.

Over the years, this memory kind of drifted away, until I started working on *Ghost Adventures*. The more involved I became with ghost hunting, the more pieces of this memory started coming back to me. It was as though investigating the spirits as part of the show had triggered my memory.

It's not like my family shunned talk of weird stuff when I was a kid. My dad had his law practice and my mom worked there too,

QUESTIONS FANS ASK

What does it feel like to have a ghost travel through you?

It feels like a wild electrical shock or charge that vibrates through your entire body. I feel goose bumps from my face down to my hands and then through my legs. A jolt like that wakes you up and heightens your senses right away. Right after, I feel a little dizzy, like my equilibrium is off.

so I spent a lot of time at Grandma's house. My grandma often spoke to me about UFOs and other paranormal topics. Grandma was especially interested in aliens and spaceships. She lived on top of one of the biggest hills in Nashua. You could see for miles around from up there. She and my grandpa had bought the house in the early 1960s during the time when a lot of people were talking about the Betty and Barney Hill UFO abduction case.

Betty and Barney Hill were from Portsmouth, a coastal city about an hour's drive from Nashua. On September 19, 1961, the Hills were returning home to Portsmouth after vacationing in Niagara Falls. While driving along Route 3 near the town of Lancaster, in the northern part of the state, the couple saw strange lights in the sky. Eventually the craft hovered so close that Barney stopped the car and they got out to look. Hill claimed that through binoculars he could see figures inside the craft that didn't quite look human. He was panicked. The couple then recall hearing a series of beeping and buzzing noises and then the next thing they remember is being in their car driving and they've traveled about thirty-five miles south from where they had stopped to observe the UFO in the road.

The Hill case became world famous. The couple had experienced missing time and a close encounter. People still talk about it in New Hampshire. I think deep down my grandma was a little jealous. I'm sure she would have wanted that same experience for herself, even if it was to validate what she suspected: that aliens have visited us before.

Not a lot of people ever knew that my grandpa worked for RCA on some of their national defense projects. He had some serious clearance and wouldn't even talk about what he did with his family. But I know he and my grandma had had some deep conversations about UFOs and extraterrestrial technology. I can only imagine the things he saw and knew.

My grandma was a smart lady. She died of a stroke when I was in college. I miss her on so many levels, but I'll never forget all those fascinating discussions we had about extraterrestrials, ghosts, and the like. She'd really thought about this stuff. She's a big part of the reason I'm interested in this subject today. My aunt Missy lived with her, and she was also into the paranormal. When I was a kid, we would all talk about what it would mean if there was life out there, and Aunt Missy had her own thoughts on the paranormal too. But she was more interested in ghosts.

At Grandma's house Missy had this creepy old doll, which she kept in her bedroom. I'll never forget it. It was an antique—brownish, made of leather, and with a little bell on its hat. When I would sleep over—on the very couch where my grandpa had died—Aunt Missy told me that the doll would walk and even run around in the middle of the night. The idea had me panicked to sleep there. There was also something about this house. Now that I've been in so many haunted places, I can look back and know what I was feeling at my grandma's. There was something there in that house. It's this feeling you get when you know there's something else present—almost like there's an electrical charge.

One time I was staying overnight sleeping on the couch, and I swear I heard the jingling of the bell on this doll's hat. It was moving around the room and throughout the house. I was frozen with fear—I pulled the blankets up to my chin, ready to duck under them to hide. Maybe it was my mind messing with me, or maybe it was real, but either way I was paralyzed. The next morning I asked Aunt Missy, "Was the doll in your room or was it somewhere else?" She let my imagination run. I know Missy was playing a trick on me, but she did believe in the supernatural. I'm sure part of her wondered if maybe the doll *had* sprung to life. To this day I'm still not sure what really happened.

From dealing with spirits so often and having had many unexplained encounters since I was a child, I've been able to piece together these paranormal pieces of my early life and figure out how they got me to where I am today. Powerful physical and emotional events like near-death experiences *do* make you more sensitive, but paying attention to the signs along the way and then focusing on the haunts is a sure way to have more ghostly experiences.

I think about these events from my life as if they were scenes from a movie. Each one builds on the last, and I'm different after each one. Little did I know back then that one day my job would involve living out my own horror movie, going from one haunted building to the next looking for answers and facing demons.

CHAPTER 2

MAKING TELEVISION

The love of my life has always been Veronique. We met in the sixth grade. The funny thing is, if I hadn't been such a problem child, I might never have met her. And if I hadn't been such a problem, I might never have been introduced to the world of video production and television. Thank God I was trouble!

St. Pat's was a Catholic school for boys and girls. I had a great teacher or two, but for the most part I don't think the school could handle me. I was basically kicked out. The principal was a nun who didn't like me because I was a hellion. I was "a distraction in class"—that's probably how she would have put it—but I just wanted to make everyone laugh. I was a smart-ass to the teachers, and always distracted. I had a hard time sitting still. I wanted to run around, climb the walls—do *anything* but sit there. I wasn't a complete punk about it, but I'm sure if I had been a teacher I wouldn't have wanted me in class.

The teachers at St. Pat's figured putting me on the soccer team would help me burn off excess energy. The soccer team was awful. They didn't score their first goal until I joined the team.

Imagine game after game not even putting up a single point. It's demoralizing. I hate losing. Plus, running around after school playing soccer wasn't enough to tame me the rest of the day. But I did love soccer—that would stay with me.

Thinking about it now, I didn't really get kicked out of St. Pat's. It wasn't exactly, "Hey, we're kicking out your son." It was more like, "Hey, you should put him in another school because he's too much trouble and we can't handle him here anymore."

I was upset because I felt I had let my parents down—I'd let myself down. I wasn't proud of being asked to leave a school. And feeling not wanted sucks. But everything happens for a reason. Although this reason would take some time to show itself. So my parents sighed and moved me from St. Pat's to public school.

It was a big change moving from a small private school where everybody knew everybody's business to a large public school. At St. Pat's I was this tough dude—I didn't worry about bullies or anybody. Pelham public school was a different story. I was the new kid, so I had to prove myself. There were bigger kids, crazier kids than me.

When I left St. Pat's, there was a girl I was dating—at least as much as you can date in fifth grade—who was two grades ahead of me (yeah, she was a real cougar). She told me that the boys at Pelham were going to try to beat me up when I got there, but she was friends with a guy who went there who would look after me.

I didn't take any shit from anyone before and I didn't plan to start now. But still, it's not cool to hear that people you haven't even met yet already hate you. I guess you could call this training ground for having a paranormal television show. It's kind of like the critics and cynics who post shit about you online after watching you on television—they don't know me, but still they

QUESTIONS FANS ASK

Are some spirits stuck here with us forever, or do they all make it to the other side?

Eventually all spirits make it to the other side. There's a reason we hear only about ghosts up to a few centuries old. We don't see the ghosts of cavemen or ancient Romans. I believe the reason is because some people are able to move on immediately, while for others it takes some time. But you need to realize there's no sense of time on the other side. So years can pass like hours. Eventually all spirits seem to figure it out and move along.

launch attacks. A tough public school will thicken your skin right up. That's a lesson you can take with you.

The Pelham kids wanted to fight me because they had heard I was the tough kid from some sissy private school. So the first thing I'm thinking about as I'm getting ready to go to Pelham is who I'm going to punch first when I walk onto the school yard.

When I arrive on the first day, I walk into the school yard holding my head up. I'm not smiling, just looking straight ahead and walking in ready for anything. Other kids are staring at me, and I'm alone. This must be what a new prisoner feels like walking into jail for the first time. It may sound like an exaggeration, but no joke—I'm thinking I'm going to get jumped. Pelham wasn't the inner city, but it wasn't far from rough towns in northern Massachusetts.

There are cliques of gangs standing around the school yard looking at me, staring me down. I've been on the school grounds for only a few seconds, and already it's a showdown.

It's moments like these when you know you can't back down. If I cower here in these few seconds, I will be cowering for as long as I'm at this school. And some people don't stop there—they spend their whole lives afraid. As for me, I'd rather get beat up and stand my ground. I knew this in that moment on the school yard.

I knew fear walking up to the school building. It hung in the air like a fog. I was young but knew I was in danger. Yet this was danger I could see—people you can fight or run away from. Now, I don't always have the fight-or-flight option. But fear is also an adrenaline rush, and I'd be lying if I said I didn't like that part of it too.

So far, no one is making a move in the school yard. It turns out I have a guardian angel here.

The guy my girlfriend had told me about was Mike Anderson. When my family had moved from Salem to Pelham, Mike's house was directly behind ours. The first day he came to my door and was like, "Hey, man. I'm Mike. They told me about what's going to happen to you when you come to school. Don't worry. I've got your back." He opened up his jacket to reveal two BB guns stuffed in there. He was acting like a gangster and shit—it was so funny. Mike and I became best friends that day and have been ever since.

So that first day on the school yard, people stared at me, but no one jumped. Mike was pretty respected in that school and he'd told everyone before I got there to just chill out. A few days later, when I started acting like a dumbass again, people started to like me and I made friends. I was getting in trouble in class, making everyone laugh, and earning some respect.

In science class I sat near a girl named Veronique. This girl stood out. She was blond and more mature than the other girls her age—she just seemed to know herself better than the rest of us. I loved making people laugh, but especially her. Making her laugh was always an objective. Though it may not sound like high comedy now, back then the shit I pulled was comedic genius worthy of *Saturday Night Live.*

The teacher would be in front of the class and I'd raise my hand and say, "Excuse me!" Mrs. LaBranche would roll her eyes because she knew I was going to do something stupid. I'd have my book open and I'd say, "I'm sorry. I just don't know what this one word means in here . . ." I'd point to my book. She'd finally walk over to my desk and look at the word I'm pointing to. "That's *A,* Nick," she'd say, then stomp back to the front of the classroom. I did this to the teacher *a lot.* Veronique thought it was hilarious. I thought she was really cool . . . I still do.

Once I got to high school, I was introduced to something St. Pat's never had: a school TV station that ran on local public access. I was intrigued.

QUESTIONS FANS ASK

When you first started out, how did you get the money to buy your equipment?

After we put together a plan for our documentary, I went to my dad and asked for a loan. It wasn't the kind of "Hey, Dad, Can I Borrow a Few Bucks?" loan, it was a "You Will Sign This Loan Agreement" loan. I had a plan to pay the money back.

I know you're thinking that's a place for A/V nerds, but I loved it. I quickly started running the channel with my buddy Danny Bedrosian, who now makes a living as a musician with George Clinton and the P-Funk All-Stars. In fact, in high school we were in a band together called Dysfunctional Family. I was the producer and wrote lyrics, while Danny was the musician. He's just amazing. He can do it all—keyboards, drums, everything—and he's a great singer too. We would bring people to my basement and put them on tape—we made a ton of those tapes, and some of them were really good!

You should have seen the videos Danny and I made for our school's TV station. I made a Mafia commercial in which I dressed up to look like the Godfather. We did that for a commercial for a new Italian restaurant that was opening up. On another video I'd follow Danny and Mike outside with the camera. We called it "'Fro Weather" because Danny kind of had a 'fro. We'd follow him around as he looked up at the sky, then back at the camera, and say something like, "It doesn't look like anything's happening today!" Okay—maybe you had to be there, but we were constantly goofing off on camera. If it made us laugh, we did it.

Everything we did was an attempt at being as different as possible. Sometimes it was just dorky friends being stupid, but sometimes it was hilarious. We would make short videos too. Mike Anderson had a VHS camera that we'd use to make videos to House of Pain music. We'd start cutting videos like that together where it was straight-up cutting from the camera—meaning no editing afterward. We would stop the camera and set up for whatever scene was to come next, so when you watched it the whole thing would flow from beginning to end. In high school

I took a telecommunications class with a really good guy, Ron, the faculty member in charge of the TV channel at the time. I learned a lot from him, like how to do deck-to-deck editing, how to run the switchboard that switches studio cameras, and how to do all the basics of television production. I got really good at it. Soon I was looking for what else I could capture on camera.

I went out and made my first short film for a psychology class project. The movie was a series of nightmares about the Robaldo family. I was drawn to dark subjects even back then.

The thing is, the Robaldo family was made up—invented by me and my friends. The film was about a guy named Antonio who owes the Robaldos a hundred thousand dollars and has to pay by tomorrow. I played the Godfather in the video. The film went into Antonio's nightmare state about what he would encounter the next day. I never forgot this idea or those characters, and I would come back to them later on.

Creating videos for the high school TV station allowed me to express myself creatively, but I guess I was pushing too many limits.

After a few too many obnoxious videos, Danny and I were banned from producing anything else. I guess some of the school administrators felt the limits we pushed were in bad taste. It didn't matter, because the fire had been lit. I loved watching movies and film, and now I had a taste for making them. I knew I'd be around video production in some way for a long time. I had to be. I couldn't imagine doing anything else—other than being a professional athlete.

CHAPTER 3

FINDING VIRGINIA CITY

During my sophomore year of high school, I had a party at my house for all of my friends. During the party I got a phone call from an ex-girlfriend, Janessa. We were good friends even after our breakup.

"I've got the perfect girl for you," Janessa told me. "You know Veronique?" I told her I did, as my memory shot back to sixth grade when I'd sat by her in science class and she laughed at my jokes. Then Janessa put Veronique on the phone and I said, "Hey, what's up?" Yup, I was smooth even back then.

Veronique and I had dated each other's friends before that, but now we found each other. I liked her right away. She was also into movies—we saw a bunch throughout high school.

One of the early movies we saw together was *Titanic*. I won't hate on the movie here, but clearly this one was for the girls—Veronique loved it. (I promise I didn't cry at the end.) But sometimes I got to pick the film. I rented Stephen King's *The Night Flier* because I wanted to see a scary movie with Veronique, the kind where you cuddle close. That movie freaked her out so much that she was seriously pissed at me for showing it to her. It took years before she'd stop talking about it.

Later we saw movies like *Memento* and *Pulp Fiction*, which blew me away by how clever the story lines were. I told Veronique I was going to make films like that one day. I was determined to see my own work on the big screen.

I didn't study much toward the end of high school. If I could wing it, I would wing it. My SATs weren't that great, but I still managed to graduate high school and get accepted to the University of Nevada, Las Vegas, to study film. I was psyched to be going into the film program, but I also wanted to play basketball and soccer for the school. Considering UNLV is a Division I school, the odds were stacked against me, but I didn't care.

My bigger concern was being so far from home. Leaving New England was going to be tough. My family was on the East Coast, along with my friends and of course Veronique, but I had to make my own way.

After high school it was a rough time for me and Veronique. I was leaving; she was staying. We didn't know what would happen between us. We agreed we'd try to do a long-distance relationship.

During the summer before my freshman year at UNLV, I qualified for a traveling soccer team. Only a few people were accepted from the United States to go to Europe to play soccer. We went from country to country and I loved the travel aspect of it. Seeing new places, meeting new people—the entire experience was thrilling for me. You think about all the people who came before you right where you're standing: the explorers, the armies, the settlers—all right there. It's no wonder there are so many haunted places in Europe.

We played games all over England, Germany, the Netherlands, Belgium, and other European countries. The games were very competitive, and I loved it. I was in the best shape of my life back then. I was gone for only a few weeks, but it was enough time to show Veronique and me what it would be like with distance between us. Veronique had already been accepted to a school in New England for business, but while I was in Europe, she reached out to UNLV.

When I came back to the U.S., I got off the plane and Veronique said, "I'm going to UNLV instead. I'm coming with you to Vegas!" Veronique had lived her whole life in New England and had been on only a few trips to places like Canada and Florida. So it was a big move. I was thrilled I would have her close by.

Since I was a kid, I had traveled to California to see my grandpa and competed in traveling sports teams all over the country. I was also used to going away to camp for weeks at a time. Travel is all I've ever known. But for Veronique, clearly this was a bigger deal.

I was so stoked. I felt like now I'd have everything in one place. I'd be playing sports and learning film, and Veronique would be there by my side.

There's a fear people have when it comes to Las Vegas. They think of gambling, prostitutes, the Mafia, the red-light district, but it's not really like that. Veronique's dad had died in a construction accident when she was one year old, so her aunts and uncles had a big influence on her growing up. Her uncles thought she was going to become a Vegas showgirl, and her aunts thought we were too young to be running away like this, but of course that wasn't what we were doing.

It did take some getting used to for Veronique. I remember

walking with her down the Vegas Strip when a homeless guy walked by carrying a bag. I thought nothing of it, but Veronique grabbed my arm like we were about to be attacked. "Are you okay?" I asked. "What's going on?" Big-city life was new to her.

Life is full of little defining moments, events that can change your course completely. Even disappointments can turn into opportunities once you look back on them.

I had everything, and I was ready to try out for the UNLV soccer team. I felt good about my chances, even though it was Division I. I was told that if I made the team I'd be redshirted as a freshman because of my less than stellar SAT scores, but I was still eligible to try.

At tryouts I ran my heart out. We had to sprint around the entire campus in 120-degree desert heat. If you didn't finish at the front of the pack, you'd be cut. I wasn't used to the temperature or the altitude—I'm used to the East Coast at sea level. These guys I was competing against were older and bigger than me. I was nineteen and could keep up with most of them, but not all. As we ran around the UNLV campus—let me just say, it's freaking huge!—I was mostly keeping up with the top four guys.

As we ran back up the last street and down to the field, it was an all-out sprint. I was in the top five and I was dying. People were almost passing out. I was about to puke from exhaustion. I've been an athlete since I was a small child and I've never gotten to the point of throwing up. But here I was dripping with sweat, pushing myself past the breaking point. *I can't do this,* I thought, but I didn't stop. My competitive nature wouldn't let me. Those four dudes at the front were insanely fast.

QUESTIONS FANS ASK

Do you need a special recorder to get EVPs, or will any recording device work?

I use an Olympus 4100PC. I'm used to it and I like the results I get. But people have had results with every kind of audio recorder—old reel-to-reel recorders, cassette recorders, mini-cassette recorders, all kinds of digital devices, even cell phones. Anything you have will work. The thing about recording EVP is that it can take some practice. That may sound strange—I mean, how hard is it to hit RECORD and ask a question? It's not technique so much as your intent and keeping at it. Eventually the spirits seem to find you.

I did everything properly. I was good—damn good. We gathered around the coach and he said, "I'm going to say who is staying and the rest of you—you're gone." He rattled off a few names, then silence.

He hadn't called my name. My shoulders slumped. I was angry and sad at the same time. I went up to the coach and said, "I don't understand what happened. You said if I came here I'd be redshirted for the first year. You'd at least give me a chance. You're not even giving me a chance right now."

He just said, "Well, your SATs weren't good." That's the only reason he could give me. I came to suspect that politics also played a big part. At a Division I school, they've already selected their players regardless of who shows up for tryouts. Finishing first in the sprint may make the coaches rethink their choice, but really they know who they want ahead of time.

I now had to face the fact that I wouldn't be on the team. A lot of kids don't realize it, but if you haven't made it in your sport by college, it isn't going to happen for you. Still, I was depressed. I wasn't cut out for Division I soccer. I was crushed. I felt like a failure.

I never have and never would give up playing sports. I still play basketball in pickup games almost weekly, but I had to accept that I didn't have a sports career ahead of me.

I rewired my brain and began to think of sports as my escape, something for fun, and I turned my full focus toward film. Back then, it was my biggest disappointment in life so far, but now I see that it was the best thing that could have happened, because it woke me up. I came to realize that film would be where I'd leave my mark.

I'd begun college as a telecommunications major, but halfway through I realized it wasn't for me. I had been working at the UNLV television station and was learning to do everything—I operated the dolly, pulled the wires, did the camera and the props. I wanted to know how to do everything in television production. There was a guy working there who really knew his shit. I went to him a lot when I wanted to learn more.

"You want to do movies and all that?" this guy asked me.

"Definitely," I responded.

"Then you need to change your major to film," he said.

That was it. I changed my major to film. The conversation we'd had was just a few seconds, but everything was so clear when he said it.

I started seeing all these other students wanting to be directors, writers, actors, editors, cinematographers. I started taking film classes, shooting on 8mm and 16mm film for projects for cinematography class, and I began learning everything about the field. I was grasping how to break out and be open-minded when it comes to visual storytelling. I think either you have it or you don't. If you can't think outside the box, you don't belong in film.

I threw myself into the subject. I learned screenplays, I learned acts, I started to grasp everything—all of the logistics involved. If you're going to capture great stories and events like haunted places and the paranormal, you need to have both the creative sense and a logistics sensibility. You may have a great idea on a camera angle or perspective, but if it requires cranes and helicopters to get that shot, it's going to be expensive and will possibly break your budget. In film, you always need a plan B. School drilled that into us, but I'd later learn just how important this concept is.

During this time I was teaching myself video editing—that's one thing I didn't learn in school. Editing takes a ton of time and focus. There's so much that goes into the process: where you cut, how you match up the video to the audio, what to leave in, what to take out, keeping the narrative moving at a good pace, building suspense, and so much more. Editing is filmmaking.

My sophomore year at UNLV was a time when I started making exciting connections. I was never much of a student, but give me a subject I love and I throw myself into it. I had my parents ship me their Hi8 camera so I could start filming more, and I was eating up everything I could on the subject.

One night at school, a film pro, who had just produced a small movie, gave a lecture about his experiences in the business. There was a fee to attend his talk, which I gladly paid. The roomful of people listened to him talk about the industry, how to

QUESTIONS FANS ASK

Is Ghost Adventures *edited? Isn't it a reality show?*

One question we often get asked about *Ghost Adventures* is about the editing. I understand the question and the concern. People who have gone out on ghost investigations know it's often not as exciting as watching a television show. Here's the reason. In our lockdown we place multiple static X-cameras that roll pretty much for eight hours. Zak, Aaron, and I also have handheld video cameras, thermal and UV cameras, plus other equipment that rolls pretty much nonstop during the lockdown. So that's dozens of hours of footage that will get turned into half the show, which is about twenty-two minutes of actual screen time on television.

During the lockdowns, hours can go by where nothing happens. We're obviously not going to bore our viewers with the misses. And sometimes our cameras or audio recorders capture something that we don't experience until we're reviewing evidence long after the lockdown is over. If we've caught something interesting, it goes into the show. If there are tense moments where one of us is experiencing something, that goes into the show. What you're seeing are the highlights from hours of investigating a location from a ton of different perspectives—mine, Zak's, and Aaron's, plus the multiple static X-cams. This needs good editing, or all of that time in between investigations would drag out more.

get projects going, and where to take them. When the talk was over, I waited to chat with him about what I was doing. I told him about the film I was trying to make and how I was going to get my own thing off the ground. I was talking this guy's ear off, until eventually it was just two of us left in the room with the filmmaker, seeking advice. The professor looked at the other guy standing there and said to him, "You want to make movies? Work with Nick." I introduced myself to the other straggler, and we shook hands.

"I'm Aaron Goodwin," he said.

Aaron and I kept talking about filmmaking. I came to find out he wasn't even a student at UNLV; he just loved film and wanted to be in the business. There are people who go to film school and there are people who are straight-up filmmakers period. Aaron is a filmmaker.

We continued talking, and he told me about this project he was working on—some funny skits called the "Aaron and Brad Show" where he and a friend walk down the Vegas Strip and do things to hurt themselves to get a laugh—like *Jackass* before *Jackass*. And I told him about this short horror film I was working on for college. I asked him if he'd be willing to help me shoot it, and he said, "Hell, yeah, I will."

So Aaron helped me on the project and we became fast friends. Our first project together was a bloody horror short. Veronique's in it too—she gets a crowbar to her back and blood comes spilling out. I would never hurt her in real life, but she was always game for being a victim in my school film projects.

It was a cool short, but I didn't understand editing back then— that takes years to develop. Nonlinear editing was just getting started and I was trying to teach myself how to use it. Most people didn't have the right computers to do this stuff then.

When you make your early projects, you think you're heading for the big time. At the time, it's the best piece of work you've ever produced. Now I can laugh at that stuff, but I had to learn, I had to grow as a visual storyteller and filmmaker, and the only way to do that is to keep plugging away.

Soon Aaron and I were getting together a lot to cut short videos. All the while we were learning how to edit.

Aaron Goodwin wasn't the only discovery I made my sopho-more year. This was also the year I found Virginia City.

With spring break coming up, Veronique and I decided to take a road trip . . . and what better place to visit than paranormal hot spots?

We drove north to some of the old haunted mining towns. We drove up into Tonopah, a town whose biggest claim to fame has always been that it's the halfway point between Reno and Las Vegas.

About a century ago, Tonopah was one of many Western boomtowns where miners flocked to look for gold and silver. At its Belmont mine, seventeen men tragically lost their lives in a fire in 1911. People said the mine, the Tonopah cemetery, and other places nearby were haunted. When you start talking to locals and you can get them to open up about ghosts, you learn a lot about a community.

Keep in mind, this was back in 2001. There weren't all the ghost hunting shows on television that we have now. Plus I wasn't on TV, so no one knew who I was back then. When I walked up to someone to ask if they knew of any haunted places, I often got funny looks. It was way different than today, when people seek me out to tell me about their local haunts.

Eventually we got some locals to open up and learned about a place called the Mizpah Hotel. We heard about a "Lady in Red" who had been seen walking the hallways and by the windows of the fifth floor. The story goes that she was a former mistress of one of the building's owners, who kept her in a suite on the fifth floor. But trouble came calling when the woman's boyfriend found out about her situation and strangled her to death in the hallway outside of her room. Apparently, she mainly haunts the fifth floor, but also makes her presence known in some of the other guest rooms.

We couldn't get inside the building because it had been shut down and closed up. So Veronique and I parked our car across the street from the Mizpah around midnight. I took out my camera and began videotaping the windows. It looked really cool, because the moon was right over the building. As I panned across the windows on the fifth floor, I saw something weird. "What the hell?" I exclaimed—you hear me say it on the videotape.

I zoomed into this thing in one of the top windows. I was like, "What is this?" I looked at it and then outside the car. I was looking for reflections, maybe a car light, maybe a neon light on a building across the road—but nothing. So I looked back and saw it start moving from one room very slowly into another room, passing the inside frames and into the next room before the glowing stopped and it disappeared. Veronique watched the same thing. On the tape you can hear us talking about this weird light. We couldn't explain it. It was wild, and I'd captured it on camera.

There we were in the parking lot staring at this anomaly, and I knew I had to get in there to look around. It would take another ten years to finally get the chance. *Ghost Adventures* filmed at the Mizpah in season five. You never stop thinking about some haunts.

After Tonopah, Veronique and I went by Area 51 near Rachel, Nevada. We drove all the way up to the fence where they'll shoot you if you go any farther. There are a bunch of zigzagging roads with small black boxes that I'm sure contain cameras and other devices. They must have known we were coming for miles before we got there. After zigging and zagging for miles, we eventually found the fence. We even saw the military jeep parked up on the hill watching us. There's a vibe there. You see the sign, the jeep, and you have no doubt that if you try something stupid, you may very well get shot. As much of a daredevil as I am, I'm not completely stupid. As I got out of the car, I wondered what would happen if I put my big toe over the line, then thought better of it. I got back into the car; we turned around, and kept driving north.

We made our way to a small town called Virginia City. As soon as we pulled into town, heading down C Street, the main drag, I could tell I was in love with the place. The mountain views are amazing, the air is clean and thin, and it feels like you've just stepped back in time a hundred years into the miner days.

Veronique and I first paid a visit to the Silver Queen Hotel. We'd heard it was haunted by a prostitute, so we asked about it in the bar. The owner looked at us a little funny. Again, this was before the ghost craze. Today when you ask for the most haunted room in a hotel, you might have to get on a waiting list because everyone wants to stay there. But back then it wasn't something the hotel promoted.

We'd barely walked into and out of the bar, and yet there was a feeling to this place I couldn't explain. We also checked out the Washoe Club. The old-time saloon and former Millionaire's Club resonated with the past. I knew I wanted to check out this place in a big way, but that would have to wait for another trip. After Washoe, we went over to the Mackay Mansion in town. At the mansion, I filmed the tour guide and asked him questions about the haunting. He told us about the ghosts of children who'd died from disease in the area, and the apparitions of some former owners, including the original owner, George Hearst. Then we went around to the various rooms. The Mackay Mansion was named after John Mackay—it was one of those Cinderella mining stories. He'd come from Dublin, Ireland, with a background in shipbuilding. He'd grabbed a pick and a shovel and soon found his fortune building mine shafts and finding gold.

Today you can go through his old haunted mansion. When Veronique and I were there, we'd heard about a haunted room where witnesses see imprints on the bed. So I sat there to film the bed. For several minutes I was just rolling on this empty bed waiting for some ghost to make an impression on the covers or something. On the tape you can hear Veronique getting aggravated, saying, "Come on, let's go!" But I was waiting to capture a ghost on film. Another minute. And another. A sigh from Veronique. Nothing happened. That's ghost investigating for you. Sometimes nothing happens.

From the Mackay Mansion, we went and checked into a small motel in town called the Sugarloaf. It was a one-story place, a serious dump. The kind of place that earns the name No-Tell Motel. But we were in college and it was what we could afford.

We went to check in and it was like some creepy scene in a cheesy movie. The guy behind the counter had one hand and looked shady. Room 1—girls can't sleep in there because a prostitute was murdered in there years ago, he told us. Bludgeoned to death. True story. When girls stay in that room, he said, they can't sleep, they say the room is freezing, and the covers get ripped off the bed.

I told him we'd take that room. "Oh, hell no!" Veronique said. "No way—I'm not going in that room!"

I laughed. Fine. So we took a different room. In the middle of the night, we awoke to hear banging on the wall. We were completely freaked out. "Is that a ghost? Is it a ghost?!" Veronique asked. She was really scared.

We heard more knocks on the wall, then what sounded like a mattress squeaking, then some other sounds that made it obvious that we were listening either to two ghosts having sex or to two living people getting freaky.

Those walls were thin! I had two pillows over my ears trying to drown out the sound. Veronique and I laughed about it, but we didn't sleep much. The next morning I went out of the room and saw this old guy coming out of the room next to us. He was outside washing his clothes in a bucket of water. How freakin' weird is that? I jumped back into the room and said to Veronique, "You'll never guess who that was! It's some creepy old guy."

We left that morning and started driving back to Vegas. As Virginia City started to fill my rearview mirror, I thought about how full the place was with history and ghost stories. I knew I would go back there again someday.

College was a great time for me. I was making connections all over the place—with people and with locations. The more I threw myself into film, the more I found my passion. Even the faculty started to notice.

As a senior at UNLV I became really good friends with the head of the film department, Professor Francisco Menendez. At the time he wanted me to help him on a new movie he was producing. His last movie had been bought by Showtime, so I was psyched to be working on his new film, *Primo*.

I was the high-definition camera technician for Menendez's movie. No one really knew how to use a high-definition camera, as it was fairly new at the time. But I was a step ahead of the game. The camera came with an attached remote control, and I was the only one who knew how to operate the thing because of the equipment training I'd had in Los Angeles. I taught everyone else. This was a real film with actors, trailers, and a budget. I knew I was going somewhere in this business right there. I even got to appear in the movie.

Menendez took a look at me on one of the days when I guess I looked a little mafioso, and he said to me, "Hey, you want to play the Russian Mafia guy really quick? Our guy didn't show up." I was like, "Hell, yeah, I do!" I ran to makeup, called Veronique and asked her to bring some of my suits over, and slicked back my hair. I had makeup give me a scar near my eye so it looked like I had been cut before. I basically created my own character right there. Spoiler alert: I die . . . quickly, in the movie. I get shot. If you ever get the chance to get shot in a movie—do it!

I had two roles on this production: camera technician and cast member. I loved being able to do it all. I knew it was just an early step. I wanted to be the guy with the ideas, the guy creating, directing, and seeing it come together.

I was taking on every project I could around this time. I worked as a production assistant, or PA, on another horror film. That's where I learned that being a PA sucks—it's like being a slave. But you should always respect the PAs, because someday they'll be somebody.

CHAPTER 4

THE *GHOST ADVENTURES* CREW COMES TOGETHER

During the winter of my senior year, I had an idea for a film project. I knew I'd need some help with this one.

I called my friend Aaron Goodwin and told him I needed to make a proposal video. "What kind of proposal?" Aaron asked.

"A wedding proposal," I told him.

The idea was a movie where I'd be traveling across the world trying to find Veronique. I would find her picture on the ground and go looking for her since I'm lost without her.

It came out really cool. We did a time-lapse effect so images fly by. We used the Vegas Strip for a lot of this because it has the New York skyline, the Eiffel Tower, the Venetian—we could walk a few blocks and make it look like we were all over the world. In a matter of minutes we could go from the Venice canals to the desert outside of town.

Toward the end I showed footage in front of a fountain in Paris because I knew Veronique had always wanted to go there. The video ends with a shot of the fountain and just holds there . . . because the video was only part of the proposal.

I'd completely edited together the mini-DV tape and I planned to give it to her on Christmas Day 2003. I had to cue the music perfectly so that when the music was playing in front of the fountain it was loud and built up, but then it would come down so you could hear me talk over it as I stepped in front of the television in person.

I wrapped up the mini-DV cassette in a toilet paper roll, so it looked weird. When Veronique opened it Christmas Day, she thought it was sweet that I'd made her a movie—she knew I didn't have a lot of money. So I made her go and watch it alone in a room. I'd had the camera already set up and everything. She thought it was really weird that she had to watch it alone, but she agreed to do it, and I went upstairs.

I timed everything perfectly so that I would come down the stairs and get on one knee in front of the television at the fountain scene at the end. By the time I got to my knee, the music had slowly lowered to background music. "Veronique, will you marry me?" I asked.

I had worked construction jobs and a ton of video jobs to save up enough money to buy a ring. My aunt worked for a jewelry store back in Nashua, so she'd helped me design it. I'd spent everything I had and had to borrow the other half of the money to pay for it. I was sweating and nervous, but I had no doubts I wanted to marry her.

Veronique said yes. I was so happy. I couldn't imagine *not* being married to Veronique.

We finished our senior year at UNLV engaged. The plan was to get married September 25, 2004.

After graduation, Veronique and I started working and then moved into an apartment in Las Vegas across the street from a basketball court. I was doing video production work on anything I could get my hands on. I filmed and edited a ton of weddings. I was working on commercials too, and I even built my own computer for editing video projects.

I wasn't making a lot of money yet, but I was getting by. Veronique was working as an event coordinator for the Ritz-Carlton in Las Vegas. Between our two incomes we were living a good life for a young couple right out of college.

Since Veronique was working at the Ritz, she was able to recommend me for a lot of wedding videos. I was working for a company that paid me two hundred dollars to film the wedding and another two hundred dollars to edit it—not a lot of

QUESTIONS FANS ASK

What does it feel like to have your own show? Did you ever dream this would happen?

When I was young I dreamed that I'd make movies one day. I did that when I was twenty-three—I made my first feature film, *Malevolence*. I had no doubts that making films was what I wanted to do. When I made the *Ghost Adventures* documentary, I had no idea it would evolve into a television show, but once we started shopping it around, a show seemed like the natural next step. Working on the television series is an amazing experience. It has made me smarter and forced me to creatively solve problems when it comes to production and capturing the stories of the locations we visit. In my heart, I'm still a filmmaker. I'm still exploring script and film opportunities—that's something that will always be a part of my life no matter what else I'm doing.

money for the job even back then, but it was steady. Because Veronique worked at this fancy hotel, we were able to hold our wedding there for almost half price.

Producing wedding videos may sound like the least exciting job in the film business, but it's a way learn a lot. Plus, so many weddings come through Vegas. I took each job as a new challenge to do something creative, to bring something new to the video. I was learning and I wouldn't take back that experience for anything.

When it came time for my own wedding, I asked Aaron to film it, and then I would do the editing myself. When Aaron got married, I did the same for him. I knew he'd do a great job with my wedding because I'd brought him on jobs before, when I was filming larger weddings that needed more than one camera. Next, Veronique and I needed to find the right music.

Not a lot of people know this, but I was a DJ in middle school to earn extra money. I DJ'd and had my band, Dysfunctional Family—I was a legend in my own mind!

I'd worked and saved so I could buy speakers, music, and everything else I'd needed as a kid. Music has always been a huge part of my life. At our wedding, I knew I wanted someone great in charge of it.

We had originally picked a DJ recommended by the Ritz, but I decided to look instead for someone cool with better music. I went online and one Web site popped up right away: Vegas Voltage. Veronique and I met with a Vegas Voltage DJ over drinks. It turned out the guy had gone to film school too and was really into movies. We liked him and hired him for our wedding. His name was Zak Bagans.

Zak and I kept in touch after Veronique and I got married.

We worked to get each other jobs at weddings, with him as DJ and me as videographer. The wedding videos were going well for me. I started a company called Artisan Wedding Videos, but it wasn't enough to make a living. Needing another job, I started working at CompUSA selling computers, which I saw as an opportunity too. I witnessed some real characters there. Everyone from the customers to my coworkers were giving me inspiration and story ideas. But the money wasn't great. I wanted to fund and pursue my own film projects, and that was going to take more money.

I was writing my own scripts for movies in my spare time. I had even produced my own feature film, *Malevolence*, during my senior year at UNLV. The film was about the Robaldo family—that old high school story revisited—but this time it had a budget and more know-how. It's funny how stories from your past come up again and again. I spent everything I had just to blow up a car in the desert. I told everyone involved, "Do this project and I'll get it screened." I didn't know how, but I knew I would do it. I was determined to see my work on the big screen.

When the project was done, I'd pushed and pulled to get it screened at the CineVegas Film Festival in 2004.

Malevolence had some weird moments in it. The film, which was partially experimental, followed a character who owed the Robaldo family a hundred thousand dollars. You saw the nightmare he went through knowing he had twenty-four hours to pay it back but no way to get the money. He knew (and the audience knew) he was going to die. Putting the movie together taught me a lot about visual storytelling—what to leave in and what to take out. There are great stories all around us. If you're going to be a creative person, you need to find a story that speaks to your gut and capture it. From that point, it's a game of finesse. You want to be visually interesting, you need to move the story along at all costs, and you need to make sure your audience gets what it wants.

Details are important, but too many slow you down. Action is important, but too much takes away from the story. Characters are critical—you need to have feelings for them (whether you love them or hate them), or the story falls flat. Teachers tell you this stuff in film school, but you can't really learn it until you actually make a movie.

Making *Malevolence* also taught me about budgeting—money, time, resources. I had friends helping me for free, people who needed to get paid, and only so many hours of daylight.

Filmmaking is a creative rush. I agonize over the edits. Do I have the right shots? From the right angles? Editing film is one of those things that seems like it's never finished. But the more you do it, the better you get. Editing makes you a better camera operator, and vice versa. Being a camera operator makes you better when you're on-screen talent because you know what your camera operator needs to get.

At the time, this film was my biggest accomplishment in video production—I had practically forgotten about those high school projects for local access TV. I felt like I'd made it—I'd got the thing screened at CineVegas. I couldn't stop smiling as I watched my work on the big screen. Now I look at this film as just another step in my career. I wanted more. I knew I could do things better.

I called Zak to talk about how to get some of my video production ideas off the ground. Zak was really business savvy and had ideas. I was sick of scraping by. I thought Zak and I could work on bigger projects, so when he wasn't DJ'ing we started filming some wedding videos together. And we were becoming cool friends.

Working together on video production, Zak and I were able to take on more work and bring in more money. When Zak came on board, we knew we wanted to do more than just wedding videos, so we started Four Reel Production Company. We were going to produce films, commercials, and other projects.

QUESTIONS FANS ASK

How does a spirit "speak" into an audio recorder? If an entity has no physical body or voice box, how does the sound get there?

While we can only guess, we think it has to do with a psychic impression. Here's a quick experiment for you. Close your eyes and imagine the voice of your mother or father. I'm sure you had no trouble hearing their voice—the tone, timbre, and inflections they use—right there in your head even though your parents may be nowhere near you right now. Maybe we know what our voices sound like and can project them energetically onto a device that can record electromagnetic information (like an audio recorder).

At the *Ocean's 11* film premiere in Vegas, we were on the red carpet filming everything. We had been hired by a video production house to film all the actors so the footage could be used for film promos and news spots around the country. We were one of many hired-gun production companies there, but it felt like the big leagues to us. We also did some big corporate videos, as well as the presentation video when Siegfried and Roy were honored by the American Heart Association. Overall we'd started to do some cool stuff and were making decent money, but we knew we ultimately wanted to do our own projects.

One night in late 2004, I was watching a paranormal show on television. I really don't remember what it was, but I do remember saying to Veronique, "How awesome would it be to go out there and see if there are ghosts and try to capture them on camera?"

She told me to do it. She knew I'd always been interested in the subject. I didn't think about it another second. I picked up the phone and called Zak. "Dude," I said, "what would you think about going out, grabbing some of this gear we have, and seeing if this ghost stuff is real?"

"That would be awesome. I'd love to do that," he replied. "You know, I had an experience in Detroit when I was a kid . . ." He then told me about seeing the ghost of a woman in his apartment in Michigan when he was growing up.

We started talking about paranormal stuff. It was just two guys throwing around ideas, but it turned into something we got serious about. We couldn't stop talking about a paranormal documentary. Zak and I would be the coinvestigators, but I knew we'd need some help. I knew different camera guys who were good shooters—they could film well—and we knew we wanted someone to have personality, because documenting what we were doing was going to be part of the process. But there weren't many people who could leave their day jobs and just take on this project for little or no pay. Nor did we have the money to pay someone the going rate. Finally I told Zak, "I know this great guy, Aaron. He's been one of my best friends for years. He'd be awesome to help do some camera work."

So I set up a time for the three of us to get together. Aaron was into it because he knew I was on board. We had our crew, I knew how to edit, and we had some camera equipment, although we were going to need more. We had the ability and the people, but we were short on one thing: cash.

I went to my parents and asked for a loan so I could buy a night vision camera, some recorders, a wireless microphone, and a new camera—a Panasonic DVX100A that had just come out. My dad said he'd lend me the money, but he expected us to pay him back. Ever the lawyer, he even drew up a contract. I thought it was funny at the time, but I realize now he was doing us another favor in addition to lending the money. He was also making the situation more businesslike. In a way, he helped us take our project more seriously, because the only way to pay him back was to make this documentary, sell it, and make some money.

Now I had the equipment, I believed in this idea, and I was willing to do whatever it took to get the project going. I was willing to quit my day job, put wedding videos aside, and just focus on this one thing. Zak was the same way. He believed in our documentary and was committed to making it a reality. With all this in place, we were ready to get started. The big question was where to start investigating.

In those early days of the documentary, Zak was coming over to my apartment regularly for meetings to plan out the project. It felt real, like we were working on a real production even though it was just the two of us and Aaron. Zak started calling potential locations to see about filming there, and I would film him on the phone for the documentary. I have hours of tape of Zak on the phone in my apartment.

It sounds crazy now, and we didn't use any of it in the documentary, but at the time my thinking was: film everything, document the entire process, because you never know what you'll need. A note to all of you aspiring filmmakers out there: a guy on the phone just isn't interesting footage.

Aaron was on the same page as me: just keep rolling the film. Keep in mind, we had no script, no notes, and not even much of a plan. We were three guys looking to investigate ghosts.

Zak and I talked at length about how the documentary should look: raw, gritty, real. Not flashy, not overly produced. This had to look like a real investigation. And real investigators don't have someone following them with a camera—real investigators film everything themselves.

We were also trying to figure out, Where do we go? Where are great haunts in Nevada? Where can we drive to? What are the unique ghost stories? My mind immediately went back to the road trip Veronique and I had taken back in college. I thought about Tonopah, Virginia City, and some of the other great old mining towns we had passed through. There was really nothing in Las Vegas for us to investigate, so we knew we had to go north.

CHAPTER 5

INVESTIGATING VIRGINIA CITY

Once we were working on the documentary, I felt excited every day. You get a feeling in your gut—a tingle that literally pushes you forward. I listen to that feeling because it means I'm heading down the right track. That rush is like a drug and I continue to seek it out as I work on new episodes of *Ghost Adventures* or other projects.

After making a bunch of phone calls to various locations, we hit the road. We filmed everything in the car too—almost all of it unusable. I filmed us singing along to stupid songs on the radio. I filmed us eating lunch. Now I can look back and can see, *This is a documentary about looking for ghosts.* What we ate for lunch isn't part of the story.

We drove all over Nevada. We hit the old mining town of Rhyolite, but didn't last there very long. We got out of the car to film something and were told by the police that we had to leave because we didn't have a film permit. I know what you're thinking: "Where is Rhyolite?" *Exactly.*

We headed farther north several hours up to Virginia City.

WHERE DID WE GET THE NAME?

Zak and I were brainstorming name ideas for the documentary. We had tons of different ideas for the name, but we knew we wanted "Ghost" in the title somewhere. One night Veronique and I were talking and thought this quest was like an adventure. I was telling Zak about it and we both said, "Ghost Adventures." As soon as we said it out loud we knew that was the title.

When we got into town, we talked our way into locations. We weren't famous at this point, just amateur filmmakers trying to appeal to people to let us go in and shoot.

I love knowing the history before I go into a location. The history gives some context to the haunting. When you look around Virginia City, it looks like the Old West—saloons, former brothels, an opera house, and it's set up there high in the mountains. It's a dry desert town with that dusty look like it's been around long enough to see some shit go down.

ABOUT VIRGINIA CITY

In 1859, two miners named Pat McLaughlin and Peter O'Riley discovered gold at the head of Six-Mile Canyon. Soon after the discovery, another miner named Henry Comstock wandered into the dig site and claimed the men were prospecting on his property. McLaughlin and O'Riley believed Comstock, and were soon swindled out of a major find. The giant vein of precious metal was named the Comstock Lode.

Soon, other miners wound their way up the canyon into the shadow of Mt. Davidson, where more gold was discovered. A tent city sprang up and hundreds of miners flocked to the region.

One of those early miners, James "Old Virginny" Finney from Virginia christened the town during a drunken celebration. The story goes that he smashed a bottle of whiskey on the dirt and rocks and called the tent city "Old Virginny Town" in his own honor.

With pounds of gold and silver leaving the earth each day in the 1860s, thousands of prospectors were drawn to the region from around the country. Soon, the silver began yielding millionaires as much as the gold, and the first industrial town of the Old West was born.

The tents soon grew into a proper city with tens of thousands of residents. There were schools, local newspapers, an opera house, hotels, and restaurants. The town's population peaked at around thirty thousand people. When you stand there today, it's difficult to imagine so many people in such a small town.

Mark Twain even spent some time in Virginia City, as a reporter for the *Territorial Enterprise* in 1863. Was this town tough? Don't take my word for it—Mark Twain himself wrote that there were so many tragedies in town from cave-ins to dead Indians that the paper never lacked material for its front page.

By 1898, the Comstock Lode had ended, and the exodus of people began. Those tens of thousands turned into a few hundred. If not for modern-day tourism, Virginia City would truly be a ghost town.

When you know the past before you begin investigating it, it not only helps you appreciate where you are and why a spot might be haunted, but it also helps you connect with the locals.

A few places wanted money for us to film inside, so we paid what we could. The Silver Queen Hotel just charged us for a room, as did the Miner's Lodge at the Gold Hill Hotel.

It was that night in the Silver Queen where the provoking style of our show was born. Zak was trying to reach the spirit of the prostitute who'd killed herself in room 11. He sat in the bathtub pretending to slit his wrists while mocking her. He told the prostitute's ghost to come and get him. I thought it was insane, but that was mostly me just egging him on. Before the camera started rolling, I told Zak, "What would you do? You're sitting in the tub, you'd slit your wrists—mocking the spirit." I know it sounds a little mean.

Here's the thing. This prostitute committed suicide. I have some tough feelings on suicide. I know these people are sick—no one in their right mind takes his or her own life—but I feel like it's a selfish way to go out. Especially when people have a family, kids, spouses, friends. Your life is all you get—that gift shouldn't be wasted no matter how bad things get.

The real provoking style came later; what went down at the Silver Queen was just an early glimpse. Provoking was really Zak's thing. It was obvious in those early shoots for the documentary that Zak was going to be our main guy—the host, the lead investigator. With his provoking, his bravado, he was the guy.

Provocation is controversial in the paranormal community because some feel it's disrespectful to the spirits, while others feel it's dangerous and can lead to spirit possession. But we were

THOUGHTS ON PROVOKING

Have you ever walked into a room where people have just been having a heated argument? Even though everyone in the room may be acting perfectly normal, there's a resonance to the room that's different. You can feel that the environment has been charged with energy. There's been an energy transfer—two people have built up rage inside of themselves and expelled it at each other. That energy will take some time to dissipate. When you're provoking spirits, you're charging the environment with your own energy. You're using words and actions that might mean something to the spirits present. That combination *will* stir paranormal events.

getting results with it, and we wanted our documentary to push the envelope. We couldn't look like the other ghost shows.

After we finished filming, Zak, Aaron, and I were sitting on a bench on C Street, just chilling and shooting some shots in which I'm walking down the middle of the street at night. These were basically B-roll shots—those camera shots you use under voice-overs or as transitions from one scene to another.

As we were sitting on the bench, all the drunks came pouring out of the bars, stumbling, tripping on the wood-plank sidewalk, and limping over to their cars. One drunk felt his way up to his motorcycle. I was thinking, *Oh, God, here we go*. I rolled the camera on him as he started off down the street, his motorcycle wobbling all over the place. Then—*bam!*—he drove right into the side of a parked car. An ambulance and the cops came to pick him up and take him off. After that, the street was quiet. Really quiet.

When a town is that quiet, you start to understand why it's a cliché that ghosts come out at night. Maybe the ghosts are around all day long too, but only when it's *that* quiet can you hear and see them without confusing the phenomenon for something else.

I then went back up to room 11 to try to get some sleep. Zak would take a shift sleeping in the bathtub, and I would get the bed. Aaron would sleep in the car, because we didn't have enough money for two hotel rooms.

Room 11 in the Silver Queen turned up some incredible evidence for us, which we showed in the documentary. Zak and I heard the sound of water filling the bathtub. It was the strangest thing. Were we hearing some phantom sound of the past, or did we get temporarily transported to the moment just before this prostitute took her own life?

The water sounds weren't the only thing we experienced. Just after four a.m. I was awoken by the sound of something at the foot of the bed. I turned my night vision camera in that direction and captured a strange mist forming right by the door just as we heard this faint knocking sound. Looking at this mist through my LCD screen, I was freaked—*It's right there, right now!* I didn't sleep the rest of the night.

The second night of our investigation was going to focus on the Miner's Lodge. The three of us set up the room with an audio recorder. Our plan was to come back and spend the night here after we'd investigated the cemetery.

Emotions and thoughts are electrical impulses in the brain, energy that radiates out from us. I believe it can get recorded right into the land. That's what I was going to look for that first night in the Miner's Lodge. Touching the spirit world, or even just the past, would be a huge adventure. I was ready for it.

ABOUT THE MINER'S LODGE

The Miner's Lodge is part of the Gold Hill Hotel that stands on the outskirts of Virginia City. Built in 1859, it's Nevada's oldest hotel. If this building could talk, it would have quite a tale to tell. It's seen just about everything, including its fair share of tragedies.

The hotel's Miner's Lodge building is the former mining office of the infamous Yellow Jacket mine. It was a place where miners would collect their pay and wash up after work, and also where the accounting books were kept.

The Yellow Jacket silver mine was discovered in the spring of 1859. The mine consisted of 957 feet of the region's Comstock Lode and produced over fourteen million dollars worth of silver.

On the morning of April 7, 1869, disaster struck when a fire broke out eight hundred feet below the surface inside the Yellow Jacket mine. When rescuers tried to enter, they were pushed back by the flames and smoke. The more the fire burned, the more poisonous smoke seeped into the nearby Crow Point and Kentucky mines. All rescuers could do at this point was to seal off sections of the mine to keep the fire from spreading. It took years of smoldering before some sections finally cooled down.

At least thirty-five miners were dead after what was the worst mining accident in Nevada history up to that point. Some bodies were never retrieved and are still down there today.

(Continued)

The only thing firefighters could do was to collapse sections of the mine to keep the fire from spreading. According to local reports, the cries of the widows who gathered near the mine's office could be heard for miles around. Some people will tell you they can still hear those cries today—a residual haunting, an echo of tragedy from the past.

One theory for the cause of the fire was that a worker left a burning candle too close to the timbers inside the mine. Another theory was that Nevada state senator William Sharon was behind an arson that was intended to close the mine for good and offer the senator a political advantage.

Whatever the cause, the result was nearly three dozen dead and a scar left on the land.

Today, just a few yards behind the Miner's Lodge, you can still see where the mine was collapsed. The lodge itself is believed to be haunted by former miners who might still be calling out for help.

When you think about this history, it helps you to tune in to the past. I start to imagine the horror of being trapped by fire. Imagine that moment when you realize you're not going to get out alive. Knowing your death is moments away must be the purest form of fear.

During investigations, we almost always use an audio recorder to try to capture electronic voice phenomena, or EVP. The idea is that spirits can imprint their voices directly on our recorders in response to questions being asked. Though you can't hear the response at the time, you hear it on the playback. This is some of the most compelling evidence we have of spirit contact.

The EVP we caught in that room at Miner's Lodge is still one of the most amazing pieces of evidence I've ever heard. You can clearly hear, "Is it the devil?" We'd let that tape roll for an hour; we hadn't expected anything, but that one quiet voice on the tape freaked us out.

As I was investigating Virginia City, I noticed a transformation taking place within me. I'm a filmmaker, a documentarian who wants to document everything I'm discovering in a raw and original way. But now, I realized, I'm part of the story—I'm in it. And not just in it—I was getting way into the investigation itself.

QUESTIONS FANS ASK

How can you be sure what you're seeing is paranormal and not your eyes playing tricks on you?

This is why it's good to have other people investigate with you or have your video camera rolling. If you see something weird, you can ask the people around you to describe what they're seeing. If it's really in the environment, then others will see it too and you can film it with your camera. You need a second opinion sometimes.

Sure, we're three friends looking for ghosts. But being there is making us something more. This experience changes you. If you don't accept the reality of ghosts, then why would you be out there looking in the first place? If you accept the possibility and start to capture little bits of evidence, you change. You become aware that there's more than the physical world around you. There's energy everywhere. People aren't just flesh and blood. Buildings aren't just bricks and wood and paint. In these early shoots, I felt that change starting.

At times I found myself nervous, or thrilled, and all kinds of other emotions. I was getting used to expressing those feelings as we were filming. We didn't have a script or formula; we were just going into these haunted places to see what happened and what we could capture.

What people don't realize is that not all the locations we've investigated made it into the documentary. When we were staying in Tonopah, we met a woman who told us about a place called the Castle House being haunted. We were told that the previous owner of the building used to hold séances on the top floor in order to communicate with the spirits there. This woman told us how local construction workers were afraid to work there after seeing a ghostly figure inside. I filmed Zak on the phone in the hotel room calling Joni Eastley, the owner of the Castle House, to see if we could get in. Joni said she was okay with it. It felt like a lucky break.

There's a shot in our documentary where we're looking out from our hotel balcony to the Castle House in the distance. In that sense, the building made the documentary. But when we investigated, not much happened.

Joni was nice—we'd interviewed her for over an hour before we investigated the basement and other parts of the building. Then we went upstairs to what they called the séance room. What made this different from the other places we had investigated was that we took more of an emotional approach. We were willing to try to feel something instead of capturing it on our equipment. When we walked into the séance room, I smelled the strong scent of perfume. Aaron smelled it too. It was our first personal experience because we couldn't figure out where the old-fashioned perfume smell was coming from.

QUESTIONS FANS ASK

Why do you think some spirits can be heard only on an audio recorder while others can be heard with our own ears?

We think it has to do with energy. For a spirit to appear in front of you in a solid-looking form takes a great deal of energy. For a spirit to appear as a misty form takes less, a disembodied voice takes a little less, and projecting energy waves onto an audio recorder takes even less. It could be that we're dealing with energy forces that aren't strong enough at that moment to do anything more than leave us an EVP recording.

The only problem was that, visually, that's not interesting. The viewer would have to take our word for it that we were really smelling something, which is why nothing from the Castle House made it into the documentary. We figured we were too new to ask viewers to trust us. If our gear didn't pick it up, if we didn't capture something on audio or video, then we weren't going to show it.

We weren't completely finished with the Castle House, though. In season five, when we investigated the Mizpah Hotel, we returned to the Castle House to see if the place was still active. We knocked, and Joni answered the door. She still remembered us after all these years.

The idea was to finish something we'd started years earlier. That evening we conducted a short investigation of Castle House. We set up in Joni's office, where she experienced the most paranormal activity. We aimed our thermal camera into the office from the kitchen; then we conducted an EVP session with Joni to try to make contact. After letting our recorders roll for a few minutes, we ended the session and climbed up to the attic—a place filled with creepy old dolls. Zak was unnerved by the dolls. He hates old dolls. I think we all do to some degree.

In the attic I suddenly felt dizzy. Then I felt goose bumps and tingles run down my arm. Behind me, I heard a loud breath right by the dolls. As quickly as the activity started, it ended. The room was quiet again and that tense energy was gone.

When we reviewed our audio, we heard what sounded like a faint conversation. One voice says, "Help"; then the other answers, "I know who you are." Joni was shocked to hear the voices too.

I loved being back in Tonopah and having the opportunity to jump back into the Castle House. Unlike the first time we went there, on this visit we captured evidence we could use.

Our *Ghost Adventures* roles weren't planned—they just fell into place. Zak naturally fell into the front-man role—he would deliver the history and story—while Aaron was always the funny one with great reactions. I was there to be the voice of reason—the one in the middle who isn't scared of much, but needs to be convinced.

Another scene we didn't include in the documentary involved Aaron and his antics. He'd walked into a candy store in Virginia City to buy a big caramel apple. I was outside filming down the wooden sidewalk and a biker couple was walking by.

Just as Aaron walks out of the store taking a bite of this huge caramel apple, the biker dude slaps his girl's ass. Aaron didn't even see the ass slap—he was concentrating on his apple. But the whole scene looked so goofy, we just cracked up. I'd put the scene in the first cut of the documentary, but in the end we dropped it. My point is, Aaron has always been Aaron—a big teddy bear of a guy with this childlike wonder and innocence about him. Whether he's trying it or not, funny stuff just happens around him.

I made a blooper reel of some of the funny things that happened to us during filming. When you're on the road, overtired, hungry, or punch-drunk, weird things happen. Today if you watch some of our video blogs for *Ghost Adventures*, you can see some of what I'm talking about.

Our style of investigating was coming together in those early documentary shoots, and we were just falling into it naturally.

One difference between what we were doing and what everyone else was doing was that we were the camera crew and producers. If you're a camera operator working on a show, your job is to film whatever the on-screen talent is doing. Your function is to focus on them and capture their actions and reactions. If the on-screen talent sees a ghost, points, and says, "Holy shit, right there!" the camera has to try to capture the reaction of the on-screen talent, and then try to film a ghost. Because we're also operating the cameras, we can point the camera at whatever we see. We stand a better chance of capturing something that way.

Our formula was starting to gel as we headed into the Washoe Club in Virginia City, a place I had never been able to get out of my head ever since the spring of 2001.

When we walked into the club, we had no idea what we were in for.

In Virginia City's heyday, millionaires were being made almost daily. The newly rich needed a place to hobnob with other wealthy men. Local establishments like the Washoe Club and the Millionaire's Club were built so the rich could drink, gamble, carouse with prostitutes, and plot ways to expand their respective empires.

The Millionaire's Club had a respectable main entrance up a winding staircase and two secret rear exits, where prostitutes could enter, and drunk and disorderly patrons could make a discreet getaway.

Inside the once decadent club were suites, gambling tables, and a billiard room. We also learned that in the winter, bodies were sometimes stored in a crypt in the building while the grave diggers waited for the ground to thaw. From raucous good times to debauchery, the Washoe Club is Virginia City's most paranormally active location.

The Washoe Club is said to be haunted by at least three ghosts: an attractive blond apparition known as the "Lady in Blue," the ghost of a scared little girl, and an old-time prospector who was known to steal unattended drinks from the bar. The drink-stealing ghost is so active that even modern-day bartenders leave out a full shot of bourbon before closing for the night . . . by morning, it is often empty.

The main bar still looks great after all these years, but when you walk up the old staircase to the upper floors, you really step back. There are no more gambling tables, furniture, bars, or even light fixtures to remind you of what used to happen here a century ago, but the rooms are still there—memories of times past still float in the air.

QUESTIONS FANS ASK

Any advice for a first-time ghost hunter?

Be careful! It's a good idea to go with someone more experienced, and be sure you're prepared: emotionally and physically. Be clean and sober, and understand that you sometimes get more than you bargain for. If you're spiritual like I am, say a prayer before you go in. And start small. A local haunted cemetery is a good place to start, or some building with a spirit that doesn't have a dangerous reputation. Document everything you do, be skeptical, but open-minded too.

The Washoe Club was the first place where I felt threatened by an unseen force. It was a skin-crawling feeling I just couldn't shake off—like something bad was waiting around the next corner.

There was a lot of area to cover in the upper floors of this building. I had set up a night vision camera in the former ballroom so it could record the entire room. I went out into the middle of the room to set up my audio recorder to try to capture some EVPs. I stepped out of the room, and something stepped in behind me soon after.

This was one of those cases where I didn't know what we had captured at the time. Back in Las Vegas I was going through tons of the footage. Trust me, it's tough to watch hours of footage with nothing happening. I was leaning on my arm watching the ballroom of the Washoe go by when suddenly I blink. Something just walked through the middle of the room! I rewind and watch again—maybe I was dreaming this. Holy shit! It's right there.

I see this semitransparent apparition walk right through the middle of the room! My jaw hung open as I watched the raw footage a second and third time. I grabbed the phone and called Zak. He raced over to see it. Zak was also floored by what he was seeing on the monitor. "Dude," he said. "Holy shit, dude!"

I knew we had something big here. This piece of evidence was the most compelling I had seen up to that point. I knew others had to see it too.

You never forget these locations, especially when you have such a personal experience or capture dramatic evidence. Such as my amazing first trip to the Washoe Club. Yet other trips there would prove more dangerous.

Washoe wasn't our last stop in Virginia City. We also paid a visit to the town cemetery. Coming from the East Coast, I just don't expect cemeteries to look like this. I'm used to lush green grass, shady trees, and simple headstones. In Virginia City the dogwoods and other trees look more menacing, more gnarled. The sand, the rocks, the rusted wrought-iron fences around the graves all painted a sorrowful picture.

Cemeteries often get a reputation for being haunted because they are places of the dead. When living people are there, we can't help but think about our own mortality. All those bodies just under your feet call out to you.

When we were walking through the cemetery, we saw strange balls of light floating around. The mood was tense. When little things start to happen as soon as you walk into a location, your senses are sharpened. Just when we'd sat down to take a breather and look around the cemetery, we heard the gravel move behind us and Zak felt something grab his shoulder.

I jumped. We all jumped. It was just reflex. We ran the hell out of the cemetery. Today I've been in this situation enough times to keep my cool a bit more, but back then this was still new to me.

Virginia City is full of spirits. Everywhere we went we ran into people who knew about them and who had experienced them. The town was our first ghost investigation success. It also scared us a bit into reality. This stuff is real, it's out there, and if we can't see it or control it, what does that mean for us? We had to keep looking.

Back in my apartment, I had a great time working on the documentary, but it was taking a toll financially. Veronique was working over eighty hours a week at the Ritz-Carlton to make ends meet, but we were still falling behind.

Our Internet was turned off so many times because we were behind on bills. I'd get on the phone and plead with the company, "We'll pay the bill!" It's kind of hard to edit and download pictures and video clips when the Internet is dead because we're behind on payment. Our cable was turned off a few times too, but the worst was yet to come.

Veronique had to get up really early to go to work. She would leave around six a.m., while I was still asleep. One morning I suddenly woke up to Veronique's scared and angry voice: "Wake up! My car was stolen!"

I jumped out of bed and went outside. I was dumbfounded. Her Honda was nowhere. So we went inside and I called the police. Over the phone the cop informed me, "Your car hasn't been stolen; it's been listed as repossessed."

We had financed the car when we were both working, and I had forgotten to pay the bills. Without a car, Veronique couldn't get to work. I drove a Toyota Echo, a college graduation gift from my parents. It was a stick shift, which Veronique didn't know how to drive. So I had to drive Veronique to and from work on the other side of town each day.

Once you start getting behind in your bills, it's so hard to catch up. Veronique and I didn't fight about the money necessarily—we weren't materialistic like that. But we were depressed because we didn't know how we were going to get by, how we were going to pay for things. I started getting down on myself, feeling like shit for not being able to bring in more income. It sucks living in your apartment and looking and just seeing dollar signs. The lights on are costing us money, the TV is costing us money, the phone rings and it's a reminder that we have a phone bill coming. Everything I see is a reminder that I need money.

QUESTIONS FANS ASK

What's it like to be alone in the dark in a haunted place with your camera as your only light source?

You'd be surprised how much you can see once your eyes adjust. But don't take my word for it. Go turn off all of the lights in your home, turn on a video camera, and start walking around. It takes about three minutes for your eyes to really adjust to the low light. After that, getting around is a little easier. But you still don't see everything. I've been cut, bruised, and bumped running into pipes, walls, debris, and all kinds of other junk that litters abandoned buildings.

When you're in that situation, being home isn't fun. There's very little escape. I was lucky that I could still go out and play in some pickup basketball games. That was still free. Sports helped me stay active and get away from the stress for a bit. Veronique had even less time to unwind. She worked almost nonstop. The only break from work she got was an occasional night out with her friends or a night in with me.

I started looking at everything in business as a hustle. I was always hustling for more jobs, more weddings, anything I could get my hands on. The problem was time. Filming took time, editing took a lot of time, and the money wasn't that great.

Things continued to spiral down for us financially and soon we couldn't afford our apartment anymore. My parents had to bail us out. We were lucky because they had recently purchased a house in Las Vegas when the housing market was good. We were able to move into the house with them while we saved up some money and got back on our feet.

We were starting to recover and got Veronique's car back. With less money stress, I could focus on the documentary again.

I had set up an editing studio in my parents' house and was ready to get back to work. Virginia City was amazing, but now we had to find someplace darker with even more paranormal activity.

CHAPTER 6

INVESTIGATING THE GOLDFIELD HOTEL

It was Zak who discovered the Goldfield Hotel while researching haunted locations for the documentary. He showed me the history of the Goldfield on my computer. I was intrigued by the tragic and gruesome story that surrounded the old hotel.

It was a little over a month after we'd returned from Virginia City, and he and I had already begun putting the early touches on the film. We were feeling pretty good about what we had, but we were also hoping to end it with a bang, something truly phenomenal. So we continued to research other potential investigations, and the Goldfield called out to Zak.

I still remember him saying, "Hey, Nick, you've got to check this out. I just found this hotel that has some dark history. Supposedly a girl named Elizabeth died chained to the radiator in room 109 and her spirit is haunting the hotel."

Now, how many similar ghostly legends are there around the country, around the world? Having researched haunted locations for many years with my cousin Justin, I had heard of hundreds of other such haunted hotels. Yet as we began to read up on

QUESTIONS FANS ASK

How come there has been no indisputable proof of the existence of ghosts?

There has been indisputable proof of the existence of ghosts. Millions of people around the world have encountered something they can't explain in any way other than to call it a ghost. Their eyes, ears, and other senses are as good as yours or mine. Likewise, I've personally captured apparitions on film, a brick flying through the air, and countless EVP recordings. The problem is that some people can't believe in ghosts, so no amount of evidence will convince them. Just like some people subscribe to a specific religion, there's no point talking to that person about any other religion. They believe what they believe and that's it.

the Internet and started talking to people about the Goldfield, it became clear that this hotel might be something unique and just what we needed to end our film—it might be the place to have a profound paranormal experience as a group.

Through a local connection we were eventually able to get in touch with the owner of the property, Edgar "Red" Roberts. It took some financial convincing—something around two thousand dollars, the last of our budget—but we were granted access for one night. At first I thought this was a pretty steep price, but later I realized they were doing a good thing with our money because it went to help renovate and restore the hotel.

I called Aaron and asked if he wanted to come along, but he had to decline because of another job, and of course he too needed to pay the bills. But I think another part of it was that

Aaron, a very religious person, had also been shaken up by his experiences in Virginia City and wasn't quite ready to face that again. For this trip, it would be just Zak and me.

After Virginia City, we had a different attitude heading into Goldfield. Our investigation style was evolving. I had a taste for this now, and I wanted more. We did a ton of research on the proper ways to conduct a paranormal investigation, but nothing would prepare us for what we were about to experience!

Zak and I loaded up my car with our equipment and headed up to Goldfield, Nevada. During that long ride, it was as if the personal and the professional parts of our identities were already becoming established. While we were on the road, we goofed around a lot and joked with each other. But then, when we were shooting, we were all business. Along the way, we filmed various scenic shots, and we even stopped and filmed an intro in front of the welcome sign to Goldfield (which we didn't use in the film). I'm not sure if what we captured on film actually expressed our feelings as we headed into Goldfield, that sort of buildup to something that we knew could have a lingering effect on our lives.

When we got into town, there was a festival going on. The town isn't highly populated, so there were more people on the street than usual. We were able to walk around town and speak with some of the locals about the Goldfield, Zak with his wireless microphone and I with a shotgun mic attached to my camera.

This is how we found out about Virginia Ridgeway, who had been the longtime caretaker of the hotel. After we'd connected with Red, he brought us to her house. Virginia was a wealth of information. I loved how organically this came together for us, which is really how the research phase should work. You talk to people and ask them who else might know something about the haunt. If they trust you, they'll pass you along to another person who may have had a supernatural experience at the location.

For us coming in as investigators, our focus is on the paranormal activity of a particular location. But to speak with someone like Virginia, whose life is so connected with the Goldfield, we were able to gain a new reverence and respect for its history.

From a documentarian point of view, it was just two guys filming the entire last thirty minutes of the film. It was just a true, raw documentary. The viewer could see the investigation unfold as we moved through the building.

We spent the daylight hours filming interviews and finding out more about the hotel. The town of Goldfield was another Nevada mining town, but gold wasn't discovered here until the twentieth century.

ABOUT GOLDFIELD

In 1902, a Shoshone Indian named Tom Fisherman walked into nearby Tonopah with some gold ore. Word spread that he'd found it about twenty-five miles north, and it didn't take long before a boomtown erupted in Goldfield. In the first six weeks of 1904 alone, the population grew from four hundred to more than a thousand.

Thousands more flocked to the region to stake a claim and work the mines for gold. Within a few short years, Goldfield

(Continued)

would become the most populous town in Nevada, with almost twenty thousand residents.

Some of those residents were quite famous. In 1904, Wyatt and Virgil Earp came to town to serve as lawmen. The Earps, those Old West legends, stood right here in Goldfield. I think about that when I'm walking through town. In fact, Virgil Earp died here—in April of 1905 he caught pneumonia and died six months later, on October 19, 1905.

In 1905, a fire wiped out a good portion of town, including the Nevada Hotel. In 1906 another fire destroyed more businesses. The dry desert air combined with driving winds meant even the smallest fires had the potential to be catastrophic. Fire leaves a mark and it destroys, but with destruction comes new opportunities.

Living in Goldfield was tumultuous. In 1907 a financial crisis led the local Consolidated Mining Company to pay its workers in scrip—paper that was good only at the company's store—with no promise that the scrip would ever be worth anything. Workers were furious; they staged a strike and took to the streets, pledging to bring mine production to a standstill. Local business owner George Winfield had enough political clout to convince Nevada senator George Nixon to wire the governor, who contacted President Roosevelt. The president agreed to send three companies of U.S. infantry into Goldfield to try to restore order. The military forced miners to get back to work. Those who didn't like the deal could quit.

Eventually labor laws would change, forcing employers to pay workers in U.S. currency, but that wouldn't be for several years. Conflicts like this led to more organized unions and employment laws; the strike in Goldfield was one of many battles in the war for fair working conditions in the United States.

In 1908 the Goldfield Hotel was built on the site of the former Nevada Hotel. The architect was George E. Holesworth, under the direction of the hotel's first owner, J. Franklin Douglas. When it opened, it featured 154 rooms with telephones, electric lights, and a heating system. The lobby was lush—mahogany furniture, gold-leaf ceilings, crystal chandeliers. A swanky place.

The boom didn't last long in Goldfield. Around 1910, the amount of gold production declined and residents started leaving. By 1920, the mines were drying up, so workers dropped their tools and headed for more golden pastures. By 1930, the town's population had fallen to less than a thousand people.

The history of a place is important to our investigation, not just a random listing of dates. If we start capturing evidence, sometimes we can line it up with one of the historical figures related to the site. If I get a name on an EVP reading, for instance, I can check it against the people we know about the site from its history, which has an effect on our approach to the investigation.

When I first walked in, I tried to envision what the Goldfield must have looked like in its heyday. I put myself into the mind-set of someone in 1908. I tried to tune in. Then I shook my head out of the temporary fog and saw the peeling paint, the dust, and the broken walls. With our daytime walk-through over, we headed back outside to get ready for the investigation.

As night fell, we made our way into the hotel, and the ominous feelings started to creep in. Just standing outside the Goldfield Hotel was overpowering. You can arrive at a location knowing all the history, but that doesn't prepare you for the energy you'll feel when you're standing right in the doorway to this dark place.

Locations like the Goldfield Hotel can draw in these negative energies. A tragic event feeds paranormal occurrences. People visit the place, learn about the tragedy, and are afraid of what might be lurking. Over time that fear compounds, creating a dark haunt.

Standing in the doorway of the Goldfield Hotel was the exact moment we first learned how to convey our emotional approach to the viewer. This is something you have to learn and keep learning, like playing an instrument. At first you learn how to make a sound, but then over time and with practice you start to create melodies that evoke an emotion in those who hear them. That's how it is with the emotions we experience on our investigations. We've gained that knowledge by experiencing them and getting better at capturing them, and over the years we've just started to pick up on things more and realized how our senses react to certain things. We wanted to be raw, to share every experience just as we experience it. We need to forget the cameras are there and just react.

Everybody reacts differently. It took time for us to realize just how we would process it all, but it all started in the doorway of the Goldfield Hotel.

This place looked just like something out of one of those horror films I'd loved my whole life. Looking up into the busted windows on the upper floors, I half expected to see Anthony Perkins in a wig staring back at me. But it wasn't just the fictional horror that was weighing on my mind, it was a good degree of actual fear. As we crossed the hotel's threshold, two thoughts were running through my head. First: *Holy shit! This is creepy! It's complete darkness in here.* But then, after a few moments, it was more: *You know, it's dark and I have only my camera light to guide me. This is awesome.*

It was that dichotomy at that moment that defined me both as an investigator and as a filmmaker.

Virginia Ridgeway led Zak and me in a séance where she became temporarily possessed. Though she seemed genuine, and you can see it all for yourself in the documentary, I'm still unsure how I felt about what was happening. Could she be caught up in the moment, or was she literally channeling a spirit? The weirdest part was the strange, unexplainable sounds going on the whole time. During the séance, I felt as if someone was lurking over us—some kind of presence was there among us.

With Virginia and Red in the building with us, I had some sense of comfort. These people knew the building and what to expect, but soon it was time for them to leave us for the night.

That's when Red locked us in—I mean, literally locked us in. For the first time, we were in a true "lockdown," which would become the signature of our investigations and our television series.

Zak and I suddenly saw what would make us stand out from everyone else. Other ghost hunters can run away if they lose their cool during an investigation. They are free to leave the haunted house if things get too intense. Not us. We wanted to face not only whatever entities were lurking inside, but our own fears as well. When the audience understands that we're trapped, the fear factor is kicked up. That fear makes us more sensitive to the paranormal. Our instincts take over. Fight or flight. In just that fleeting moment, we inadvertently found what would differentiate us from all the other paranormal seekers. There's a big difference when you can't simply walk out the door, no matter how intense things get. And things were about to go beyond intense in the Goldfield Hotel.

Once I heard that final lock click into place, that's when the adrenaline really kicked in. *We're trapped inside.* I kept hoping we'd get something—after all, we'd spent some pretty good money to get into the place. We didn't have all that much left, and I was praying we'd capture something significant and not just a bunch of useless footage. The price we'd paid turned out to be a bargain.

Our motive throughout the entire shoot was to keep it raw. It was just the two of us, and that was what the investigation would be—nothing fancy, no camera tricks or odd angles, just straight documentation. We'd been reading up on proper investigation techniques and theories, and at the time orbs were the big thing. The strange balls of lights in photographs that show up on film but aren't seen with the naked eye, which some people think are a sign of paranormal activity, are still controversial today.

Personally, I think that 98 percent of orbs can be thrown out and attributed to water vapor, dusts, lens flare, and all that crap we now know. But when you've spent years looking at orbs, you start to realize that not all of them can be so easily explained. When orbs appear in conjunction with other paranormal activity, that remaining 2 percent can only be described as balls of energy. I think true orbs are just that: energy. The paranormal is an open book, and there are new things to be discovered every day.

At that time, orbs were new to us, so we thought taking pictures throughout the Goldfield would be beneficial. As more and more things started showing up on film, there came a point when we were getting scared. Yet there's nothing wrong with being scared on an investigation. It heightens your senses and perhaps makes you more in tune with your surroundings. It certainly did for me that night.

It's not like there was a catalyst for the fear at this point. I felt my pulse quicken, felt a tingling sensation on the back of my neck, and sensed something ominous. There was no reason to have these feelings yet, but there they were. In the coming years I'd learn to pay close attention to those feelings when they happen.

As I was walking around shooting on my Panasonic DVX100A, Zak was ahead of me taking pictures. I followed him as we went down the hallway, past room 109, and up the stairs.

Room 109 was the room the locals had told us about again and again. The story goes that a prostitute named Elizabeth was chained to a pipe in the room and was killed there because she had become pregnant with the child of a former Goldfield owner. The owner had supposedly chained Elizabeth in this room until the baby was born, then took the newborn and threw it down an old mineshaft in the basement. He left Elizabeth to starve to death. When Zak first walked into the room, he immediately got chills.

As Zak was taking pictures, I was filming him, yet the whole time I could feel something following me. All I kept thinking was, *If there is something following me, when is it going to finally attack me?* These are the types of thoughts that go through your head.

Finally, I slowly turned the camera around to see if there really was anything behind me. Then I had to turn the camera a little more so the dim light from the LCD screen would shine down the pitch-black hallway to show me whether something really was standing there. You're essentially putting all your faith, all your safety and sanity, in the light of a tiny LCD screen. For me, it's still one of the creepiest moments in the documentary.

The activity intensified as the night went on. When we investigated the upper floors later on in the night, we captured a figure that was peeking around the corner and then just disappeared. We first saw it with our own eyes, although Zak had a better view of it from where he was. I didn't completely buy it until I reviewed the footage. When I saw it captured on film, that's when it got me, when I knew it wasn't just my eyes playing tricks.

Even when I see something, my mind immediately begins trying to logically explain it. It's just how I keep myself balanced, always trying to put an explanation on something. But when

QUESTIONS FANS ASK

Can you sense that a place is haunted before you begin an investigation?

I'm not a psychically sensitive person, but that doesn't mean I don't occasionally feel some force around me. When the hair stands up on the back of my neck, or if I feel a cold spot, I pay close attention. In most locations, I don't get much of a sense of the place until paranormal phenomena start happening. But once in a while, in a place like Linda Vista, I walk in and am on alert from the first minute. Our bodies are the best piece of ghost investigation equipment you can ever have.

something that is hard and factual evidence is being validated on a piece of equipment, you just can't wrap your head around it. So you have to come to terms with it, and that pumps you up to keep searching for the answers. That was a big moment for me.

The night was getting more intense as we pressed on. We soon made our way down to the basement after hearing the sound of something metallic dropping onto the floor. I was tired and scared, and Zak and I kept getting separated from each other. The basement was so dark. I was thinking about the strange things we'd already seen and heard, and I wondered where I would run in an emergency. A hundred thoughts were going through my head at once, but one thought stood above all others: *Just keep filming.*

Another strange bang on a pipe somewhere behind us, and we're now totally on edge. After Zak and I collect ourselves, we make our way down the passageway following the glow of our night vision cameras. We pan around the corner into a room and come to another dusty room. Our cameras settle on some debris for only a second when we see a brick levitate and launch across the room—all of it captured on tape.

At that moment, I panic. We both do. If some invisible force can throw a brick, then it can hurt us. That thought races through my head in the same instant my body is already turning to run.

The flying-brick moment is the biggest event in the entire documentary, and it's the evidence for which we have become best known. And despite what others have tried to say for years now, it's 100 percent legitimate.

A lot of people like to point to an edit cut in the footage, but everything is in real time. What you see there is a cut from one camera to the other, and I'll take you through the entire sequence of events that led up to what I feel is historic evidence of the paranormal.

Just prior to entering that portion of the basement, Zak was like, "Hey, we're going to confront this thing." Later, when we were about to enter that room, he said, "Nick, you going in first?"

I could understand Zak's apprehension, because prior to that, the activity had already been amping up in the basement. As I was walking through the complete darkness, I was looking at where I was walking using the LCD screen. From the moment we stepped off the staircase, we could tell the environment had shifted.

After a while, it just felt as if we were walking underwater, just a very heavy feeling. As we walked down the creepy hallway peering into rooms, the banging sounds suddenly got louder. That's when we both started to get nervous. In the film, you hear Zak suggest I sit down for a second, and I respond, "I'm not sitting down. I don't know where I am. I'm not, you know— Why would I sit down?" It's funny what comes out of people's mouths when they're nervous.

Eventually, we gathered up enough courage and adrenaline to push forward and search out whatever was making those sounds. That's when Zak suggested I go into the room first, but I wasn't having any of that. So the shot you see is actually the view from Zak's camera; then it switches to mine, so you can see the brick from the best angle. And it wasn't just the brick—other items were being thrown; scraps of metal were flying. This was true poltergeist activity. When you're confronted with that— something you've never experienced before—everyone is going to react differently. I don't care how tough you are—it's a scary moment. Being new to the paranormal, we reacted the way we did: we ran. Zak went blazing out of the room, and as I took off after him, I was surrounded by this completely weird feeling.

I lost him in the dark and began drifting off in a hazy fog, like I was only partly conscious, wandering through rooms on my own. I lost myself in the moment, enveloped by this strange energy that seemed to be guiding me. I had no idea what was going on, and total confusion had set in. I wasn't even aware until watching the footage that Zak had run upstairs and then come back down to find me. That's when I had the creepiest moment of anything we'd caught on film—I realized I should have heard him calling for me, but I hadn't. I'd never responded.

Perhaps something had control of me, keeping me from hearing Zak call out to me. I think I didn't hear him because I was so scared, I just didn't know what to do. I didn't know if I was going to get attacked, if something else was down there with us. I imagine it's kind of like being behind enemy lines—maybe that's the best way to describe it. If you're behind enemy lines in combat, you're not going to start yelling out to your fellow soldier and give up your location.

I was totally drained of energy, and I was scared that if I called out to Zak, I would give myself away. I might get thrown or clawed or something terrible like that. And when we reviewed the footage, we caught a disembodied voice saying my name—so it knew just where I was. You hear it say "Nick" and then there is a burst of energy that fluctuates across the frequencies. It was the first time I heard an entity say my name, but it would not be the last.

We captured a similar disembodied voice on Zak's camera just before he shut it off, which I believe he did accidentally—he must have been shaking so much he accidentally hit STOP on his recorder.

We knew then that it was time to get the hell out of there. But with the doors locked, the only way out was off the second-floor fire escape. A lot of people have accused us of making up that part of the story, saying there's no way we could have survived a two-story jump unscathed. But you've got to consider a couple things—first, we were in good shape, pretty athletic, and it wasn't as big a fall as you might think. The other thing was that our fight-or-flight instinct had kicked in. People are able to do some pretty amazing things when faced with danger. If a mother can lift a car off a baby pinned underneath it, then it was no big deal for me and Zak to jump off a second-floor balcony.

Of course, it's different now. Over time you learn how to get out of certain situations. And now we're locked into locations all the time, so we're used to it. These days I let the shit hit the fan, but right then I just wanted to get out of there as fast as possible.

When we got in the car and took off, it was around five a.m. The day was beginning to dawn, and at that point we'd been up for twenty-eight hours straight, between driving up there and filming, and now we were on the road back home. We were about three hours out of Las Vegas when I began blacking out as I was driving. Zak was already in a deep sleep, and I began drifting on the highway.

I pulled over and told Zak I couldn't drive anymore, that we should just sleep in the car for a while. He said he could drive, no problem, but then he started drifting off while driving as well. Finally I made him pull over again and I drove the rest of the way. That's why today we have a production crew member drive us after a long night of investigating.

Once we got home, I slept for an entire day before I started going through the footage. What I saw blew my mind. Zak and

I reviewed everything over and over again; it seemed we must have watched it a million times. We began showing it to family and friends, and they had the same reaction. We knew we'd hit it big. We'd found something that we had to show the entire world.

But we also knew that what we had was going to be scrutinized from every angle. I thought it was important to get other people's opinions and put them on camera. That's when Zak found Victor H. S. Kwong, a physics professor at UNLV, to analyze the footage of the moving brick. When he couldn't explain it away with his vast knowledge of physics, that just made the footage that much more impactful. We also had Slim Ritchie, who has an impressive background in the video profession, take a look. He analyzed the video through a variety of filters and programs and stated on camera that he saw no evidence of tampering or trickery.

That was what we needed. We needed others' input to give it gravitas. We were the ones who'd experienced it, so our analysis might be somewhat skewed. We felt it was important to bring in a third party to analyze moments like those, and over the years on the series we've done it more and more. Even though we've become much sharper at analyzing things ourselves, it's always good to get other people's opinions.

But even authenticating what happened to us didn't have as much impact as when we went back to Goldfield and showed our footage to Virginia. She said what we'd documented with our equipment was pretty much the same type of phenomena that she herself had experienced there for years.

As we were leaving Goldfield for the last time, the thought came to me for a final climactic scene of Zak walking through the Goldfield cemetery. It proved to be just another weird moment in a series of weird moments that would always happen when we film *Ghost Adventures*. We found a grave with ELIZABETH engraved on the headstone, and at that moment we saw a sort of rainbow forming over the town that seemed to go directly toward her grave. I knew it was an amazing moment, so I set up the camera as fast as I could. Then I swung the camera around just in time to capture a cool flash of lightning. We were getting these amazing cinematic shots, and we felt they would close the documentary off perfectly.

The Goldfield experience definitely had a lingering effect on me, and it became the basis of what the *Ghost Adventures* series would become. But it also became our paranormal proving ground, the place where the evidence we captured would forever be either put on a pedestal or dragged through the garbage. It thickened our skins as investigators for our experience that night in the hotel, and it thickened our skins as researchers for the slings and arrows our evidence has endured.

Back when we first started showing our documentary to people, I would get frustrated when they didn't believe it was authentic. It's sort of like if you've painted a picture, but then everyone tells you it's too good to have been painted by you. That's what's so frustrating to all paranormal investigators—if someone hasn't experienced it themselves, you're never going to fully convince them of what you've captured on film.

Looking back, maybe I was that way before we started making the documentary. Maybe I myself would have said, "Wow, that's cool, but I don't necessarily buy your story." But now, having had my own experiences, I really listen to the thousands of people who want to share their own ghost experiences with me. Everywhere we go, someone has a story to tell. Now I listen and, instead of judging, I embrace. It's their experience and it happened to them, and it has meaning to them. It's exactly what happened to me at the Goldfield Hotel.

The only difference is, I had it all on film.

CHAPTER 7

EDITING AND THEN SELLING THE DOCUMENTARY

O nce filming was completed, the real work began. It was time to take our adventures and turn them into a coherent, linear story and begin the process of editing all the footage together.

I had built my own computer, and I had my own editing software and an editing deck with a small TV monitor. How I'd rigged it all together was very complex, and I was the only one who knew how to use it all properly. Video production has come a long way in just a few years, but back then what I had rigged worked for what I needed it to do.

I asked my buddy Mike Mouracade, who'd written the music for *Malevolence*, to create music to amp up some of the more suspenseful moments in the documentary. Zak and I felt it was important for the viewer to feel what we'd gone through emotionally, and music would help express that.

I also had to balance all the audio and edit together all the takes. Add in the time it would take to capture the video footage to the computer's hard drive, and it's easy to see why it took a good, long time for it all to come together.

Zak came over every day and we would work on it together, including writing the whole narrative. We would brainstorm, script the voice-overs, and then Zak would go into the bathroom to record them. While it wasn't exactly Skywalker Sound, it got the job done.

I got a rush showing Zak some of the cool montages I'd put together. One example was during the Goldfield segment, when we were conducting the séance. I really wanted to paint a visual image of what we were experiencing emotionally, so I overlaid visual shots over the séance footage to convey what we were going through. It was very complex and took a lot of time, but the result was well worth the effort. I felt I was able to bring the viewer into that séance with us.

Looking back, I realize it was one of the craziest projects I've ever worked on in my life. It certainly took a ton of effort and resources. Some mornings I'd wake up and get right to work without even taking a quick shower. Veronique would come home and find me still unshowered, still editing, looking like a zombie in front of the computer monitor. When I look at the *Ghost Adventures* series now, I find it amazing how far we've come.

But it was about to get even crazier.

I'm not saying the original documentary was cursed, but there was an unusual energy surrounding the entire project. Even during the editing process, strange things began to happen. Some of it may have been my own fault—at that time, I didn't see the value in backing up my video editing projects because it took too much time. That was lazy of me, and I would pay the price later. Always trying to cut corners and get things done quicker, I thought that since I knew the technology so well, the technology would never fail me.

Boy, was I wrong.

While editing the documentary, I had four 300GB external hard drives all linked together and tied into my computer with one FireWire cable. I was too cheap to go out and get more FireWire cables. To this day I'm not exactly sure what happened, but I think I unplugged the FireWire cable from the first hard drive and tried to plug it into another. That interrupted the flow of data to the computer, and essentially crashed the hard drives. Every time I tried to open the timeline for the project, the screen would read, FILE LOST—ALL CORRUPTED.

Anyone who has ever had a computer crash and kill a huge project knows how this feels. I went into a rage, kicking myself for not being more careful. There's no worse anger than when you're mad at yourself.

I would have to start from the beginning and work it out like a puzzle, figuring out what piece was missing so I could get the project to open up. But panic began to set in when after the tenth time trying to reopen it—after restarting the computer, restarting the hard drives, and whatever else I could think of—still nothing happened.

Finally, I just called Zak and said, "You know, I've got a problem. I don't have any of the timeline from point A to point B of the documentary. All the shit we put together is gone."

I was panicking, saying over and over that I didn't know what to do. Zak just kept uttering an occasional "What?" I wasn't sure if he was confused or if he thought it was a big joke. I ended the conversation by telling him to just bear with me, that I would figure it out.

I hung up the phone and spent the next few minutes bitching and moaning, but then started going through a process to evaluate everything. I started crossing out the lines and trying different things. To be honest, I don't know how I did it, but I was able to rig one hard drive to another and get the project to open. It was still corrupted and I had to rework some things, but in the end I salvaged the film and you'd never know there had been any issue. The one major loss was a blooper reel I'd cut—that one I never got back after the crash. I wish I still had it. It would have been one for YouTube for sure.

In a way, I'm glad the crash happened. No good lessons are learned without some significant pain. When you're faced with losing hundreds of hours of work, you get a good scare and a reminder to be more careful in the future.

Aaron wasn't involved much with the editing because he had to move on to some of his other film projects. When he would come over to hang out, I'd show him different clips and get his feedback. He dug what we were doing, but at the same time the experience had freaked him out. He wasn't interested in reliving some of those moments any more than he had to.

Other weird things happened early on as we were putting together the documentary. Once we felt the film was ready, I thought it would be cool to have a screening at my parents' house and invite over some of the neighbors. I wanted them there because our closest friends already knew about the experiences and what we'd captured. I wanted to bring in new people who didn't know, and see the expressions on their faces when it all played out on the screen.

We created a spooky atmosphere, lighting some candles around the room and turning off the lights. We placed speakers atop the television. About halfway through the film, the speakers inexplicably flew off the TV, hitting the candles and sending wax flying everywhere. The neighbors got up and left the house, they were so scared. Some of them later told me they had nightmares after that, and others felt like something had followed them home.

Now, I don't know if what happened was anything truly paranormal. It could have been something as mundane as the vibration of the bass causing the speakers to move. But the undeniable fact was that our film had made an impact, even on the people who saw it first.

After everyone else had left scared, the only people remaining were me, Aaron, Zak, and Veronique. I had kind of planned it out so that once we were done watching our film, I could turn on a television special that was coming on about Bobby Mackey's Music World and the haunting there. The legend was that there was a portal to hell in the basement of this former animal slaughterhouse, because there was a satanic cult that performed rituals there many years ago. Plus there was the ghost of Johanna, the daughter of a former owner who'd killed herself in the building. I had to know more about this place. My cousin Justin loved digging into the past of haunted and notorious buildings. After all the research we had done into this place, I knew it would be the perfect fit for another adventure. Even while I was editing our documentary, I would show clips to Justin and he would keep reminding me about Bobby Mackey's.

I told Zak and Aaron that we had to go check the place out, but even after they watched the television special, they didn't seem that excited about it. Their response was basically, "Well, you know, whatever . . ."

I couldn't believe they were being so dismissive of a location that was obviously a great fit for our vision. But we eventually made it there, and it turned out Zak and Aaron had some of their craziest personal experiences there. But that wouldn't come until much later. At this point, all we had was a rough cut of a documentary that a handful of people had seen.

During the documentary editing process, things in our apartment were getting really tough. Veronique and I were broke. That was the point at which we had to move into my parents' house in Las Vegas. We were bummed out to be losing our own space, but I knew we'd get back on our feet as soon as I finished and sold this documentary.

The first room I unpacked and set up in my parents' house was my editing studio so I could get right back to work.

Sitting in my new studio, I wondered how we were ever going to get this thing in front of people. We had this unbelievable footage. We had an apparition caught on camera, the brick at the Goldfield Hotel, this poltergeist activity. Yet I was starting to panic that the only people who were going to see it were the media in Las Vegas. While I continued to work on editing, we'd put our first rough cut out to some local media. *Vegas Weekly* reviewed the documentary and liked it, and the local Fox affiliate had us on their news program for an interview. But nothing came out of that. No big breaks.

I tried to enter the documentary into all the major film festivals, like CineVegas, Sundance, and so on, but it was turned down. We did, however, make it to some of the smaller events and even picked up some accolades. We won the Grand Jury Prize for "Best Documentary Feature" from the New York International Independent Film and Video Festival in 2006, and we were nominated for "Best Feature Film" at the Eerie Horror Film Festival that same year.

I knew smaller film festivals wouldn't be enough. We'd need an agent to get it out there. This was a powerful documentary; everyone needed to see it. So I started hustling. I looked up hundreds of agents online, then went down the list and called each one. I heard all kinds of responses:

"Send it to us to review."

"Do you have representation?"

"Have your lawyer send it to us."

"No, thanks."

After a few of these phone calls, I got better at pitching it over the phone. No agent wants to deal with someone who doesn't know what they're doing—which is why breaking into the business is so hard. But I learned the business end of things fast.

My phone calls went from "Hey, could you maybe look at my documentary and represent me?" to "I have this amazing documentary. Some of the most compelling paranormal footage ever caught on tape. It's already won awards at film festivals."

I noticed the conversations with the agents were getting longer and more interesting.

I was on the twelfth page of agents when I had a guy say, "All right, sounds interesting. Why don't you come to LA tomorrow and show it to me." I agreed. Then I was like, *Fuck. How the hell am I going to do that?* But you don't say no to an opportunity like that. I called Zak and convinced him to meet me at my house early the next morning.

At the time I was working for a place called Cashman doing wedding videos. I had to walk in and tell my boss, "Look—you know that documentary project I told you about? I need to take tomorrow off because I'm going to meet with this agent."

"If you do that, you might get fired," he said.

I told him I understood, but I had to do this. It was too big of an opportunity. In the end, he respected me for following my dream, and let me off the hook.

Zak and I hopped into my Echo and drove all the way to LA. We got to this house on Mulholland Drive—weird, like in a David Lynch movie. We walked up to the giant mansion and knocked on the door, but there was no answer. "Hello? Hellooo?" we were saying. Finally someone came out and told us the agent wasn't here. I called him on his cell phone and he told me we'd have to come back later.

Zak and I were pissed. We began arguing—we'd just wasted a four-hour drive from Las Vegas for nothing. We weren't going to just leave the DVD there, so we decided to head over to Universal Studios and go on rides the rest of the day. Finally, late at night I got a call back from the agent telling us to come over.

It was late, but we headed back to his house and played the tape for him in his living room. We sat there and watched the whole thing with him. He said he liked it. "I'm in," he said, but he wanted us to recut it this way and that way. We agreed, and back to Vegas we went.

We worked on trimming some of the fat from the film, eliminating a lot of the on-the-road footage and much of what were our attempts at humor. Looking back, we realized nobody thought we were as funny as we thought we were.

In cutting all that stuff, we really brought the film back to its original core: the pursuit of the paranormal. Without the goofy stuff, the scare factor was really amped up. We knew that was what would make people want to watch it.

I mailed the revised documentary back to LA.

The agent introduced us to a distribution company that had

a lot of ins with various networks. The distributors took the project and brought it to the SciFi Channel (which is how they spelled it back in 2006) as well as a few other places, but it was SciFi that showed the most interest. I couldn't believe it. We had a shot at getting this thing on television on a real network!

At this point, we were talking about trying to get it released as a DVD or a limited run in select theaters. We didn't know exactly what the best route was; we just knew we wanted people to see it. Zak and I were making phone calls constantly, dealing with a lot of hang-ups and rejection along the way. Finally, we got a response from our distribution company. SciFi was interested!

At the time, SciFi was looking for programming to follow their own paranormal shows, and they loved our film. They thought it would fit right in.

During this time, Veronique and I were on the move again. This time to Laguna Beach, California. I thought it would be good to live closer to Hollywood, and Veronique was able to get transferred to another Ritz-Carlton hotel out there. Life in California wasn't easier for me, though; I was still commuting to Las Vegas to film weddings.

SciFi had picked up the documentary for seven air dates, and it did extremely well. The first night it ran, it drew a 1.7 rating, which is huge for a cable network. Close to two million people had tuned in to watch it, and the responses we heard were amazing. Everyone loved the fact that we were new, we were underground, and we were different from the other paranormal programming they were used to.

When it aired, we had a party and everybody got together to watch it on TV. I thought it was pretty awesome to see ourselves on television—and not only in the documentary itself, but also in all the trailers and promos that SciFi had put together to promote it. Our film did so well, they even aired it an eighth time, one more than our contract had stipulated. (For anyone out there planning to sign a television contract, read the fine print!)

We were by no means TV stars at this point. From time to time I did get recognized on the street, but I still had to work my regular job. Nor did we really make much money from the SciFi deal—it made it easier to pay some of our bills, sure, but it wasn't life-changing. In fact, we didn't even pay back all our loans until well into season two of the *Ghost Adventures* series.

Once the film aired on the SciFi Channel, it just took off. It was all over the Internet. Back then, MySpace was very popular, and we promoted it all over there. By the time people were seeing it at the festivals, they already knew all about the film and were already fans. It was around this time that we started putting together the Ghost Adventures Crew, or GAC, an organization of like-minded paranormal investigators and fans of the film. We began taking those folks out on ghost hunts as well. It was a way to bring people to the locations where we'd experienced our paranormal encounters in the documentary. We wanted people to have the same experiences as us. Though it took a little convincing, Aaron agreed to be a part of the events. He was ready to get back into the haunts.

Even as we watched the documentary over and over again, we never really saw things we wanted to change. We stood behind our film, and people liked what they were seeing. From our provoking style of investigation to the raw feel of the film, it was a hit on every level.

Well . . . except for one guy. To be honest, it was the only criticism I can remember. In a magazine article, some guy bashed us on every little detail of the film, including our provocation. It was pretty harsh. Our intention was never to piss anyone off. It was just to find our own way in the paranormal and take those who wanted to watch along for the ride. Unfortunately, though, most people are only going to love you or hate you. That's a tough lesson to learn. There are still times when I dwell on the negative things I read online or in print. Even if it's one complaint for every hundred compliments, it's tough to not think about that one.

With all these successful showings on SciFi, we continued promoting ourselves online as best we could. We had about ten thousand friends on MySpace—a far cry from the two-million-plus followers *Ghost Adventures* now has on Facebook—and we were constantly filming small vignettes and posting them on YouTube, which was just starting to hit big around that time. From there, various media outlets found out about us, and soon we were the darlings of the paranormal television world.

Even as we were basking in the success we had created, we also had to start looking forward. Would we continue doing more documentaries? Would this concept have a life as a weekly television series? Zak's brother-in-law knew a guy who knew a guy who owned a production company and had an in at a couple of networks. Sometimes, that really is the only way to get a foot in the door. So we stuck our feet out firmly and met with the guy in New York City . . . Maybe this documentary, this team of Zak, Aaron, and myself was destined for our own series. The circumstances that had brought us together were strange enough, but now something bigger was brewing on the horizon.

CHAPTER 8

SELLING THE SERIES

When we were pitching ourselves to television networks, all we really had was a loose outline of what we wanted the show to be. We wanted the main focus to be the investigations themselves, but we'd also include the history, background, and a walk-through tour of the locations, as well as interviews with historians and witnesses to paranormal phenomena. Those were the essential elements, which we would need to turn into a formula. The three of us—Zak, Aaron, and myself—pitched the series as something that would always be real, always be raw. I didn't know yet about a "sizzle reel," which is a short version of your intended show that you put together to wow network executives and give them an idea of what it would be about, but I knew enough to cobble together some of our best moments of footage from the documentary along with some footage of the GAC events we'd filmed. It was four and a half minutes of the best of what we were all about.

Eventually, we had a meeting with Travel Channel. We sat in a huge room with a very large table in the center, dominated by a gargantuan monitor. I felt like we were sitting in Frank Cross's office in *Scrooged*, all spread out around the table and pitching to just this one guy. After visiting so many networks, we had become kind of nonchalant about the whole thing, not as gung ho as we might have been when we were first starting out.

We started talking with this exec, telling him about the film. Right as Zak was in the middle of the pitch, the guy got up and said, "Hold on a second." He'd just seen a friend of his walking by the door, someone named Matt Butler, a guy who would change our lives.

The exec told Matt he had to come check out our film. As it turned out, Matt is really into the paranormal—he's the guy who brought *Most Haunted* from British television over to the Travel Channel in the United States.

So we all watched the DVD together. When it was over, Matt said, "Wow, that's amazing. Awesome." We could tell he was really into it. We started talking more about it, and when we saw his enthusiasm, it really gave us a good feeling about where the meeting was going. We'd come so far doing everything we'd done—all the craziness that had led up to this moment. I tried to express that to Matt as best I could, and I could see he understood. There was a moment where I felt like we just connected, almost as if I had known this guy for a long time. We were all kindred souls, and the whole thing started taking on an "it was meant to be" feeling, which we so often hear about but so infrequently experience.

We left the meeting feeling great. Since it was one of our first times in New York, the three of us decided to head over to the Statue of Liberty. It was while we were waiting for the boat that we got the phone call from the production company that had set up our pitch meeting.

They basically said, "Travel Channel is really interested. They gave us an offer. They want to do it. They're going to give us eight episodes." And our response was, "Hell, yeah!" Before this point, we'd had offers from Discovery, Biography, and some other networks, but they all wanted us to film a pilot. We felt we had essentially done that already with the documentary. Travel Channel was offering the promise of something real—eight episodes—and that was the opportunity we truly wanted.

We got to the Statue of Liberty feeling like we owned New York, even after exhausting ourselves climbing all those stairs to the top. As we stood there and admired the expanse of the world around us, I could feel like it was ours for the taking. After all our hard work, opportunity had come knocking. But now, instead of just opening the door, we had to invite it in, make it feel at home, even cook it dinner. It wasn't going to be an easy undertaking turning our ghost adventures into a series, but nothing worthwhile ever is.

Right away I thought about how now we could explore Bobby Mackey's Music World, Moundsville Penitentiary, and all those other places my cousin Justin and I had been researching for the last couple of years in the hopes of filming a second documentary. We could investigate the paranormal on our terms, gain access to the places where others might not dare to go. It was all happening the way I'd dreamed.

We headed back into Manhattan to the Travel Channel offices to begin breaking down just how the series would work, and we signed all the necessary paperwork. All these suits were asking us questions like whether we were members of the Screen Actors Guild. A lot of "reality" shows out there today feature out-of-work actors sporting SAG cards, but that wasn't us. We were just three dudes who'd made our own documentary, financed it ourselves, and devoted ourselves fully to it. And the executives were very happy about that.

But at the same time, they were taking a huge chance. We were three unknowns, both in the paranormal world and in the world of television and filmmaking. This was in the years following 9/11, when there was a lot of economic uncertainty. The job market, the housing market—nothing was stable. Yet this network believed enough in what we could do to give us this amazing opportunity.

They saw us as three individuals who could work well together with no bullshit, and what you saw was what you got. I think Matt Butler was a big push behind it, and we later became good friends. One night we were hanging out together in a bar in New York. He told me that what had really sold him on the series was that flying brick. So whatever that malevolent force was trying to do when it launched the brick at us, it probably didn't have the intended effect.

Now we would be coming at those dark forces armed with a renewed sense of purpose. We had better paranormal equipment, better filmmaking equipment, and a better budget. It would still be just three guys locked into these locations hunting down the unknown. But now we didn't have to worry about all the other distractions we'd had to concern ourselves with when we'd filmed the documentary.

It was 2008. I was twenty-eight years old and getting ready to produce a television series for a major cable network. Yet I wasn't really concerned, not even when they pushed contracts and numerous other binding legal documents in my face. As far as I was concerned, that was all just business. I wanted to get that part over with so I could move on to what I love. I knew in my heart that I was ready for this leap.

The series was going to be different from our documentary. We wanted to keep the raw feel, but a television show needs structure. We couldn't just make up the narrative as we went along.

Sounds easy, right?

The show would also no longer be just me, Zak, and Aaron on these investigations putting together the show. There would be other crew members and production people involved—a prospect we found both exciting and daunting at the same time. We knew we still wanted the investigations to feature just the three of us, but we'd have to learn to put our trust in a whole bunch of strangers and hope they would stay true to our vision.

The production group who works on our show is small, and everyone has to do a lot of different things. Because Zak, Aaron, and I would be wearing multiple hats for the production, we really needed a first-rate researcher to help us with all the background. We needed someone who could do the research and the write-ups for a location, then make the phone calls to secure interviews with people there. This was going to be an important job, because it would all have to happen well before our team arrived to film. So we couldn't trust it to just anyone.

We looked at a couple of people for the job. We reached out to my cousin Justin since he'd been such a big help so far, but he couldn't do it because he had a job already.

Zak got in touch with radio personality Dave Schrader, who we really trusted. When the documentary had come out, we'd done ghost hunting events in Virginia City and Goldfield with Dave. These were some of our first Ghost Adventures Crew events. I liked Dave from the start, but I was unsure of what he actually wanted. He would tell me things like, "Be careful of the people you work with in this industry," and to watch out for this or that. Why did he care so much about helping us out? What was his endgame?

In Goldfield, Dave and I had been chilling one night, having drinks together. We started laughing and having a good time, and that was when I realized Dave really was a cool guy. I could let my guard down around him and put my trust in him. We became good friends from then on.

So when Zak asked Dave who would make a really great researcher for the series, he had one guy in mind: Jeff Belanger. At the time, Jeff had spent almost a decade running Ghostvillage. com, one of the world's most popular ghost Web sites. He had written nearly a dozen books on the paranormal and combined a healthy respect for the history of a location with a keen sense of who the people are who have had the paranormal experiences there. He was the perfect fit.

We ended up working with some really outstanding people the first season, like Hugh Hansen, our production supervisor, Anthony DiDonato, our line producer, and Joseph Taglieri, one of our producers. Kathy DaSilva would come out into the field with us to help create the reenactments, along with Christian Hoagland, who is an awesome cinematographer. We really got to know each other and became a tight little mini-family when we were on the road.

On the first day of filming a location, we shoot our interviews during the day, plus B-roll shots. The B-roll is for those great-looking shots that don't necessarily show action, but are a stylized look at the building or the space inside. On the second day on location we get to spend some time in the town hanging out with locals. It's during this time that the production crew really gets to know each other.

The first location we filmed was the West Virginia State Penitentiary in Moundsville, West Virginia—or just "Moundsville," as most people in the region call it. Moundsville wasn't the first episode to air—that was Bobby Mackey's Music World—but this old prison was the first we filmed.

Working on the series was a lot different from filming the documentary, when we really didn't have a time limit. With the *Ghost Adventures* series, we had four days to film a whole episode—interviews, reenactments, lockdown, and reaction. We had new equipment; the entire industry was making the move to high definition, and we had to follow suit. We could no longer use the cameras we'd used to shoot the documentary because they didn't meet network standards. Instead, we were given state-of-the-art Sony cameras that took mini-DV tapes and had XLR inputs so Aaron and I could monitor the sound ourselves. I would monitor the audio from Zak's mic, and Aaron would monitor the audio of whoever Zak was interviewing.

I had to make sure I knew what I was doing. I didn't even get the new cameras until the day before we were supposed to leave for Moundsville. I had them shipped to my house and tried to read the manual as quickly as possible so I could be ready for filming just a few days later.

We were responsible for getting the cameras to the locations too. We had to carry them with us on flights and keep them with us wherever we went. It wasn't enough that we already had to worry about our own stuff. Now we had to worry about transporting and protecting these very expensive cameras! Just ensuring the equipment got from one place to another might have been more nerve-racking then heading into a reportedly haunted building. If you think the TV business is glamorous, it often isn't!

I was constantly concerned about whether or not we actually *would* capture any paranormal activity at these places. Many people felt that what we had caught in our documentary was a once-in-a-lifetime kind of evidence, and now we were going to go and seek it out *eight more times*? I had all the confidence in the world that we could make a well-produced, visually appealing documentation of the quest for the paranormal. I had little confidence that the paranormal would comply.

A lot of debate went into the locations we chose. We had many meetings and discussions about different places. We had our own ideas; our production team had their favorite haunts— there was a lot of back-and-forth. Our criteria for a location: It had to be huge. It had to have dark history. It had to look scary. And, of course, it had to be haunted. Not just with friendly ghosts either. We wanted to know (living) people were scared inside this place, that they felt threatened. Where else could you go for all that evil than an old prison? Moundsville's history was downright badass.

Bad people in a bad place is a recipe for a dark haunting. We were ready to tackle Moundsville.

As I mentioned earlier, I had experiences I couldn't explain when I was a kid. They were enough to let me know there's more out there than what we see every day. I'll never be able to explain the apparition we captured in the Washoe Club or the brick flying in Goldfield, but I still wasn't completely convinced that all this stuff was for real. Maybe it's a power of our mind?

ABOUT MOUNDSVILLE PENITENTIARY

Nine hundred ninety-eight men died inside this prison's walls. Dozens were hung, several electrocuted, many more murdered by other prisoners. Then there were those who couldn't take the sentence of prison living and committed suicide to escape.

These stone walls have seen hard men broken, dreams shattered, and evil punished.

The death and carnage at this West Virginia penitentiary have left a mark that can never be washed away. By many accounts, some of the tortured souls who served time under this roof are said to still lurk in the shadows of the prison walls.

The story of Moundsville's penitentiary began in 1863, when West Virginia seceded from Virginia to side with the Union in the Civil War. The newly formed state needed a prison, and the close proximity to the then capital of Wheeling made the tiny village of Moundsville the perfect location.

Between 1866 and 1876, prisoners sentenced to hard labor toiled stone by stone to construct the ten-acre prison. The work was oftentimes grueling, especially in the hot West Virginia summers.

When the penitentiary opened in 1876, it brought an influx of jobs to Moundsville. The village grew and job opportunities at the prison helped the locals, but the downside was sharing their peaceful landscape with the worst criminals in the state—including the ever present threat of jailbreaks.

Life inside the walls of the West Virginia State Penitentiary was hard. Moundsville had the dubious honor of being on the U.S. Department of Justice's list of top ten most violent correctional facilities during its 119-year history.

Maybe it's something else entirely? No matter—I wanted to come face-to-face with something that could end the debate for me. I wasn't afraid of anything paranormal when I left Las Vegas on April 14, 2008, heading for this tiny West Virginia town. I was psyched to get started on the series, but I was overthinking everything. I wanted the shoot to go perfectly.

Veronique gave me a big kiss, said "good luck," and I was off to the airport. The entire plane ride I thought about our new equipment, and the angles I wanted to take on the building. I thought about our investigation—how we needed to capture not only our evidence, but also how we were feeling. Because that's the most important part of a television show: capturing the emotions of the moment. When you're out in the middle of the night alone in a haunted place, you go through a roller coaster of emotions. There are tense moments, and there are also funny times when you're spooked by something stupid like the wind or a mouse running by. The whole point was to capture all of that.

When we landed, I picked up our rental car. Zak, Aaron, and I started making our way down through West Virginia toward Moundsville.

I wanted to keep everything as real and raw as possible, so we pulled over in a restaurant parking lot across from the jail to get our gear set up. I wanted Aaron to film our reactions the first time we drove up to the building. I was driving the car and trying to figure out which street to take to get there. As we rolled closer, we felt the sheer presence of the prison.

The place was huge. Like some old green-stoned castle. Dark, even on the bright sunny day we arrived.

We were still in documentary mode when we arrived, because that's what we knew. When you film a documentary, you film everything from every angle. You film and film and film, and you edit later.

When we arrived in West Virginia, I was feeling the pressure. When we filmed our documentary, there had been no timetable. We filmed when we could, we edited when we could, and we had all the time in the world to get it just right.

In West Virginia we had to get everything shot in four days. Not only that, but we had to do so with completely new equipment. We now had real-deal hardware—wireless mics, great cameras—but this also meant we weren't yet experts on how the gear worked. When we rolled up into the small town of Moundsville, I was sweating. I remembered how much work the documentary had been, and now we were about to do it all again—eight times in a row! There were people depending on us, and tight deadlines, but also the opportunity to make a dream come true: our own television series.

Back in our first season, we were still filming on digital tapes. I laugh when I think about how many we used in Moundsville. If I was walking to the next room during the daytime interviews, I filmed it. If Zak was eating lunch, I filmed it. The cameras never stopped rolling.

We spent the first day of the shoot walking up to the houses across the street from Moundsville and knocking on doors asking if people there had had any paranormal experiences. These locals were so down-to-earth. Many of them used to work in the prison. They were happy living where they did, even though they were less than a football field away from this scary building. One family was huge—all these people living in one small house. They invited Zak, Aaron, and me to play baseball with them. Here we were playing baseball with this family right in the shadow of one of the most haunted places in the United States. It was surreal. We filmed part of the game, but we didn't air it on the show because it didn't have much to do with the story. But we had fun.

We also had some inevitable arguments while filming that first episode. Aaron and I were the main camera operators that first season for the daytime interviews. It was up to us to capture every moment. Though we knew each other, we still had to get used to working together as a team in a fast-paced shoot. People were scheduled for interviews, so there wasn't much time to practice.

We were just about to film the first interview when Aaron and I exchanged some words. I white-balanced my camera off a nearby wall. When you white-balance, you're making an adjustment to your camera so white looks white and colors look natural. If you ever look at a picture or video and everything looks bluish or kind of orange, there's a good chance the camera wasn't white-balanced. If you're using multiple cameras, this is really important because as you cut from one camera to the other, it has to look like the same camera shot—otherwise it's jarring to the viewer. And to try to fix a mistake like this in postproduction is a serious pain in the ass.

Aaron white-balanced his camera and put it next to mine so we were pointing in the same direction. I could see his shot looked orange while mine looked more crisp.

"Your white balance is off," I said.

"Dude, I just did it . . . *Yours* is off," Aaron said.

We bickered back and forth, and Zak asked what was going on. I was pissed. Aaron was pissed. And we were losing time. As we each rechecked our settings, together we realized that we were both kind of wrong. We can laugh about it now, but at the time we were pretty angry. We glared at each other throughout the next interview.

Messing with each other during the shoots is a tradition on *Ghost Adventures*. When you're using multiple cameras, you need some kind of visual and audio cue so you can sync everything up during editing. If you've ever seen any depiction of a Hollywood movie being made, you've surely seen someone walk in front of the cameras with a marker board with a handwritten scene and sequence. They clap down the top of it with a snap; then the director yells, "Action!"

The idea is the same, but we don't need a fancy marker board. Aaron and I both roll our cameras on Zak and ask him to clap his hands. It accomplishes the same thing—our editor then lines up each tape on the visual of the clap and the sound.

"Okay, Zak . . . give me the clap," I said.

"I'm not sure if you'll get it, Nick . . . I may not be contagious," Zak said.

Zak clapped.

"I didn't get it," I lied. "Give me another clap."

Sometimes we see how many times we can make Zak clap before he stops.

On that first shoot, we had our challenges too. Right from the start, things didn't go exactly as planned. When we knocked on the door of an elderly gentleman who lived across the street from the prison, he fainted while talking to us. Literally, he fell right over. I thought he had died!

Someone dying on camera wouldn't have been the first time for me either. Years ago, on a wedding shoot, I went to get a close-up of the father of the bride or groom (I can't remember which), who was having a great time dancing, smiling and everything. I got in for the close-up shot and then *boom!* The guy collapsed right there on the floor from a heart attack. You can imagine how tough it was to edit *that* wedding footage together.

Thank God the guy in Moundsville woke back up a few moments later; he just had low blood sugar or something.

Since we have only four days to capture everything on these shoots, we plan what we can, but we also want to leave room for things to unfold organically. There was one lucky moment when we were getting ready to go inside the jail to film, and Tom "Redbone" Richardson, a former inmate of the prison for almost twenty years, just happened to be driving by and stopped to see what we were doing. He ended up giving us an amazing tour with an insider's perspective that we never would have thought to seek out on our own.

Even as we were filming for the first time, I was trying to think of ways in which we could make our mark, differentiate ourselves from other paranormal investigators. I was thinking about possible experiments, different things we could do to push the limits of both filmmaking and investigating. How could we do it better than everyone else?

I wanted to break the rules of paranormal investigation. You never get anywhere doing the same thing over and over. One of those paranormal rules is: don't go in alone.

Sure, there are a couple of good reasons for that rule. First, safety: if you get hurt, you might need another person to get help or get you out of there. But also, if you witness something paranormal while you're alone, it's tough to know if your mind is playing tricks on you or if there's actually a presence in the environment. A second witness could verify this for you.

The reason I'm comfortable with breaking this rule is that the two other guys know where I'm going and can come help me if I need them. Plus, I have my camera and audio recorder. If something is in the environment, my gear will be my second witness. But my biggest reason for wanting to go it alone was that Aaron and Zak were both hesitant. So I said, "Screw it. I'll go."

While in the dark basement of this old and deadly prison, I wanted to go into the "Sugar Shack" by myself. This place is one of the most infamous rooms in the complex. The prisoner recreation room was better known among the inmates as the "Sugar Shack" because it was here that illegal activities like gambling, fights, and murder took place, but also rape; hence, it was a place for the cons to "get some sugar."

We'd learned that guards didn't want to be down here with the inmates because of the horrors that went on. It may sound odd, but those of us who have never been to prison have a difficult time understanding that the value of life inside is different from the value outside. When you have no freedom, no money, and no family, your life can be devalued down to a pack of cigarettes.

QUESTIONS FANS ASK

Do you guys ever get scared before going into haunted places?

Most of the time I'm psyched to go in. We've done the research, we've heard from the eyewitnesses—and sometimes the victims—of the entities inside, and now I want to experience the location for myself. But once in a while, there's something so ominous about a place that I do get creeped out. Linda Vista Hospital was one location where I felt myself gulp before going in.

Guards know that, though, because they live a dual life—they live the life on the inside with the inmates, but they also get to go home at night and appreciate their families, homes, and other luxuries foreign to those serving time.

I was ready to put my own stamp on our investigations, and going into the Sugar Shack alone was the way to do it. No other show had done anything like it. Early on in the series, that became my calling card—it was always "Let's stick Nick in the morgue" or "We'll send Nick in here alone."

After hearing all the stories about the Sugar Shack, I wanted to experience the place for myself. It was crazy to hear the graphic material that came from the prison guard we'd interviewed who used to work there, but the stories "Redbone" told us were even creepier. He told us about a riot in which a prisoner was found with his penis cut off and shoved in his mouth because the other inmates thought he was a snitch.

As I sat there alone in the Sugar Shack, those gruesome details kept going through my mind. I wondered if the spirits there would prove to be as demented and angry as the people who once inhabited the prison. These thoughts would enter my brain and mess with my head until I started to really get scared down there in the dark on my own. I kept hearing noises, like something was moving around. I couldn't see anything, and I've never been the kind of guy who walks around with a flashlight. All I had was my LCD screen, so I could see a few feet in front of me in the dark, but that was it. It was at this moment that the paranormal, our investigations, and the *Ghost Adventures* series started to get real for me. My heart rate was speeding up and I was sweating a bit. I was afraid something was going to attack me and I wouldn't know where it was coming from until it was too late.

The scariest moment for me at Moundsville never even made it into the episode. For another solo venture during the lockdown, I went up to the prison hospital on the second floor all alone. As I roamed throughout the rooms and hallways, I could actually hear disembodied voices that sounded like they belonged to the inmate patients of another time. However, those sounds weren't recorded on my digital audio recorder or camera. Let me tell you, that place was *haunted*. The problem was, most of what proved it to me were just feelings, and we had better-documented material that ended up making the show. I'm not an actor, and I'm not good at pretending. If I have a genuine reaction to something, that will make it in the show. If it's just a creepy feeling, that's not enough.

When we left Moundsville and got home to go through our footage, the real challenge began. We had hours of tape from several different cameras. We wanted to show the best parts of the lockdown, and not just footage of us walking around talking about what we were feeling. We had to capture our investigation and cut it down to about half the show—thirty minutes of screen time, but only twenty-two minutes of footage without the commercials—showing only the best of what we encountered. On those first few episodes especially, what to cut and what to keep was always a difficult decision.

It was during those first edits that we learned that sometimes there are tense moments we want to keep in the show, and other times there are moments when we've caught evidence even though we didn't realize it at the time. Once we'd reviewed our audio recorders and mini-DV tapes, we found the anomalies and then had to fit them into the lockdown segment.

That first lockdown was really draining. I think I slept the entire day after I got home to Vegas. I was amped up to investigate, and I was working hard to get everything right now that the stakes were so much higher. Now I could rest—but only for a day, since we still had to edit.

Think of it like this: You're a basketball player trying to help your team win the championship game. You give everything you have—your heart, your soul, your ability—and you leave it all out on the court. After that, you're drained.

The buildup of emotion of getting to the championship game, and then the buildup of being broken down whether you've lost or won—those are the same feelings that we go through during a lockdown. There's the buildup of being there, hearing things, and then going in and battling it. Some locations are worse than others, and can just drain your energy just by your presence. The lockdowns really screw with your emotions, your energy, and your body, and it takes at least a weekend to gain it all back—sometimes even as long as a week. After the episode where we returned to the Goldfield Hotel, I was out of commission for two weeks. I felt nauseated, like some entity had attached itself to me. It took a long time to shake it off.

Resting was a luxury when we started filming. Doing the investigation and filming everything was only half the battle. We would comb through the audio and video looking for anything that might be considered evidence. We were worried about being able to deliver, to have something profound come out of every episode, until we realized that that's not what paranormal investigation is about. If we didn't capture anything while we were filming, maybe we'd find it during our analysis. If we didn't find anything then, maybe it was emotional experiences that we could share. At the end of the day, it's not up to us to determine whether or not a place is haunted. Our job is to share our experiences during the course of an investigation. We set a strict policy of "no bullshit": no weird camera tricks, no "What was that?" moment where we pretend to hear something off camera. What you see is what you get.

QUESTIONS FANS ASK

Were you just being melodramatic for the camera at Moon River Brewery?

I'm not a good actor. I tried years ago in my own film, *Malevolence*. I had two lines and I wouldn't hire myself as an actor again. You'd be surprised how fast you forget about the camera once you work on a television show. Maybe in those first couple of episodes in the first season I thought about how I looked or sounded on the camera, but those thoughts are distracting. Now when we start investigating, the camera is just an extension of me. I'm doing what I do whether the camera is on or not. I don't hold back, and I don't turn it up either.

Something else that sets us apart from other paranormal shows: we're not only the series creators and the guys on cameras, we're the camera crew and the editors as well. We can't blame our editors for making us look bad (or good, for that matter). It's all on us to deliver.

In other words, once the show began, my life became—well, I had no life. Not that I'm complaining, but everything became about the show. Our routine became: investigate, film, analyze, edit, and then move on to the next one. I had to capture all the footage onto the computer, go through it, and organize it. My whole life, I had been a PC guy, but when we started doing the show we had to move everything to Mac so it could be edited in Final Cut instead of Adobe Premiere Pro, which is what I was used to. So I had to learn a whole new computer operating system in addition to different editing software.

Though all three of us had to adjust to the hectic new schedule, Aaron was the luckiest. Once the investigation was finished, he could go home and rest. Zak and I had to edit.

The editing process involved cutting the footage and laying it all out, an ordeal since we had all those cameras and digital recorders to deal with. I had to mix all the audio from the three cameras. I had no assistant to help me with any of it that first season—I had to do it all. And then Zak would come in and make suggestions, so we had to restructure it in a way we both could agree on. Sometimes, we had to agree to disagree.

I spent late nights in the office, past midnight sometimes, just by myself. Zak is okay with sleeping until the afternoon, but I'm an early riser. So those late nights were killing me. Veronique would bring me food at night, or we'd meet somewhere so I could grab a quick bite and get back to work. And then finally, when I had the lockdown portion edited down to half the episode, I shipped it off to New York. The New York production group would then add the other half of the show—the great camera shots that opened each episode, the interviews, and the daytime tour of the locations. We were basically shipping hard drives back and forth.

This just wasn't what I had imagined. With our documentary, of course, we'd had to do everything ourselves. I was naive and thought that once we got a television series we'd have tons of money and a huge staff doing all of this for us, but that isn't how it works. You need to get into this field because you love it. And not just the investigating—that part is easy to love. You need to love every part of the process, right down to the evidence review, the editing, the tiny details that go into making a kick-ass show.

CHAPTER 9

THE TV ADVENTURE BEGINS

It didn't take long for tensions to begin to mount while shooting the first season of *Ghost Adventures*. For one thing, we had only those four days to shoot an entire episode—interviews, walk-throughs, research, and the lockdown. We got one shot at doing everything and getting it right. That's a lot of pressure, especially when it's your first time producing a television series.

Another problem was that whenever the three of us were together, strange things would happen that we hadn't planned for in our production schedule. An elderly man passing out when he answers the door. A former inmate pulling up as we head into the prison. My name being called at the Washoe Club. These things turned out to be some of the most memorable moments of the show, but they also threw off our shooting schedule.

We never know what we're going to find, and things rarely go the way we've envisioned. That's what makes filming *Ghost Adventures* so interesting. Every time I go to a location, it's always different from the last one: the people, the environment, the situation, the filming—and that's not even including the paranormal encounters.

But things going awry can often lead to increased drama behind the scenes too.

Zak, Aaron, and I are three different personalities, but ultimately we all click well together. We love what we do, we're passionate about it, and nothing could ever change that. But being on the road, and being around each other—we're all creative types who have strong feelings on how the show should look—we're bound to have some tense moments. You know the old saying "Familiarity breeds contempt"? Well, it's true. Family members, friends, college roommates, even rock bands suffer from it—when you're around someone so much, you start picking up on all their little annoyances, and it becomes amplified. Something small gets blown up into something big, and those tensions eventually boil over.

I've noticed that the energy of the location can have an effect on how we interact with one another while filming. For example, at the Houghton Mansion in North Adams, Massachusetts, the third episode we filmed. You could feel a kind of sad presence there. That melancholy force may have had a role in the heated argument Zak and I got into right before our lockdown.

On August 1, 1914, Albert Charles Houghton was out for a ride with his daughter Mary and two family friends up north. In the small town of Pownal, Vermont, John Widders, their chauffeur, tried to steer their new Pierce-Arrow around a horse-drawn carriage. Widders pulled the car too far toward the side of the road, where the wheels hit some soft dirt and sent the car rolling down the embankment. Everyone except Mary Houghton was thrown from the car. Family friend Sybil Hutton, one of the other passengers, was killed when the car rolled on top of her. Mary was badly injured, and she died later at the hospital in North Adams. Widders was so upset that the next morning he walked to the Houghtons' barn and shot himself. Though Houghton himself wasn't injured in the crash, his heart was broken. He died about a week after his daughter. This tragedy left a sad mark on the mansion. We believe that John Widders and A. C. Houghton still haunt the home where they once lived and worked.

It's possible that all of the sad energy that has built up can take an emotional toll on the place. I'm not saying that this location is completely to blame for what happened between Zak and me, but it could have played a part.

The argument started because I didn't put a wireless microphone on Zak before the lockdown began. I assumed that he could do that himself, but he assumed I would do it for him. Neither of us was right and neither was wrong, but it just escalated into a shouting match between us. We should have just suited him up with the microphone and moved on, but instead the tension that had been building came to a head and we were yelling at each other.

As anyone knows from watching *Ghost Adventures*, Zak has a strong personality. He knows it, and he doesn't shy away from it. But Aaron and I also know a different side to Zak than you'll see on TV. One of the questions I am constantly asked is why I allow Zak to tell me to "shut up" all the time. There are many instances in early episodes where he tells Aaron or me to be quiet. But it's not that he wouldn't allow us to have our say; it's just that Zak is in the moment of the investigation, and he's so involved and engulfed that he doesn't really mean it as harshly as it comes across. Normally he might say, "Hey, guys, just be quiet for a second, okay?" But when the shit is going down, when paranormal activity appears to be happening, Zak is on edge and his words just come across a little more sharply than he might intend.

My approach to investigating is to listen more than speak, but it's inevitable that you're going to have to tell the other two guys to shut up at some point. Aaron and I handle it differently than Zak—everyone has their own way about them—and as a result it sometimes looks like Zak is being rude to us on investigations.

That comes to a head sometimes, as it did at the Houghton Mansion. So Zak and I yelled at each other, but the issue, of course, wasn't the wireless mic—it was everything. As we were in each other's faces, every thought went through my mind: Are we going to come to blows? Is this the end of the show? Do I want to keep putting up with this shit?

No punches were thrown. After the standoff we both walked away for a minute to collect ourselves, while poor Aaron was left running back and forth trying to calm us down. We were under pressure we hadn't been under before, but we both quickly saw we had a job to do, and we both wanted to check out this haunted mansion. I'm glad we yelled at each other—it broke the tension and made things better in the end. At the end of the day we looked at it as a brotherly bond.

Late in filming season one, Zak realized how it was coming across when he told Aaron and me to shut up, so we started taking a lot of it out in the edit. We thought it made Zak look bad even though we knew it wasn't personal; it was easier to take it out than to constantly have to address it. And over time,

Zak became more chill as an investigator. As we did it more and more, he became less on edge and more mellowed out. It was just part of the learning curve for all of us.

People who want to parody Zak—and there are some good impressions out there, as even he'll admit—will always say, "Shut up! Shut up! Shut up!" They'll also throw in repeated use of the words "dude" and "bro," which, actually, all three of us are guilty of overusing. Some people have even made a drinking game out of it—every time one of us says "dude" or "bro" in an episode, they take a drink. Good luck with that! Play that game and you'll probably be toast before we even get to the lockdown!

Dude, when we're in the moment and forget there are cameras on us, that's what we become. We say it a lot and it just flows from us, especially in moments when we're not exactly thinking about what we're saying and are instead focused on what we're experiencing. When we filmed in Tucson, we had to trim out so many "dudes" in editing that it even annoyed us, bro.

The way we talk and react is, I'm sure, part of the reason I've received so many compliments over the years on the show. People perceive us as genuine. If you go through some big-time experience, your reaction probably won't sound like a Shakespeare sonnet. It's more like, "Wha . . . wha . . . what the fuck was that?!"

During the filming at the Houghton Mansion, some of the executives from Travel Channel showed up to check out the operation. Matt Butler was one of them, and even though we had become friendly, I was still a little intimidated by all these network people hanging around. It only added to the stress between Zak and me, since we wanted to impress those guys and show them we were pros.

I wasn't a network person; I wasn't even all that familiar with the television industry. When Matt started asking questions about the Houghton Mansion, about its history and the reported paranormal experiences, I felt more like a kid facing a pop quiz. It turned out the guy was just interested in the place and what we were doing. I realize now that his questions were just the kinds of questions we needed to answer for our viewing audience through the course of the show. Working with the Travel Channel helped us evolve our project in a big way.

I wanted to impress the network execs, but I also wanted to stay true to our original vision for the series. After signing on, we had meetings with the network about what we wanted the direction of the show to be. One of the biggest things I told everyone when we first started the series was that I never wanted our show to go "Hollywood," to become some big production. It's easy to get caught up with bigger budgets and want to do fancy effects, but I wanted it to stay raw, because that's what made viewers connect with our documentary in the first place. I thought it made for more gripping storytelling from a filmmaker's point of view, and it would be more true to an actual paranormal investigation.

The paranormal research groups that go out and investigate film all that stuff on their own. There's no big camera crew following them around, no audio technicians, and they don't just hand off the tapes to some editor who compiles them into a television show. If we had a polished Hollywood-style show, it would take away from the true nature of paranormal investigation.

We wanted to be in charge of 99.9 percent of our own stuff. We wanted to do our thing and keep it raw. How could we trust the editing hand of someone who wasn't there? How could we trust them to know what is paranormal and what isn't? Even for us, it took a long time to figure out what was truly paranormal evidence. It takes a lot of research; we had to develop the skills to discern what is anomalous. In season one, you probably saw a lot of orbs and stuff like that, which could have been spirit, but could just as likely have been dust, bugs, water vapor, or some other mundane crap. The reality is we're always learning.

Now I've definitely become better at figuring out true anomalies from natural phenomena. I do believe there are orbs that are indeed balls of energy or are indicative of spirits. I get thousands of people e-mailing me or sending me pictures on Facebook asking me, "Can you tell me if this is an orb or just dust?" Most of the time, I have to tell them it's just dust.

When checking out an anomalous photo, I can tell if it's something incredible or not right away. I do have to admit, there are some that have made me sit up and take notice. With some of the more interesting images, I'll get a little more in-depth with the person who sent it, asking what they think it is. A lot of people will say, "Well, my family member died there and I captured this. Could it be that family member?"

In my experience, a genuine orb produces its own light. On video it might flutter or pulsate; on a still picture it would light up the area around it. These are rare, but do happen.

My response when someone shows me an orb picture is always the same: I wasn't there, I don't know the conditions of how it was captured, so it's hard to say. But if you think it is Aunt Sally, then maybe it is.

That's the problem: you don't know who or what you're dealing with. The person who took the picture could have emotional issues as a result of the death of a loved one. There are a lot of people who just need validation for what they think they've captured, and because I'm on television, they think my opinion matters more. I'm a stickler about it—I ask very blunt questions, like whether or not there was a flash, or a window that might cause reflection. I'm straight up with folks, which some people appreciate, but others don't. But it's just too hard to be sure something is paranormal, and I don't want someone running around with a doctored photo claiming it got the "Nick Groff Stamp of Approval" (no such stamp exists anyway). I have to protect my name and my integrity as a paranormal investigator, something I learned early on in filming season one.

I know how easy it is with today's technology to digitally "add" ghosts into photos. You can do it pretty easily with Photoshop, and there are a number of smartphone apps that will automatically do it for you.

To help us decipher truly unexplained audio, video, and photographic anomalies, we reached out to, and soon became friends with, several known experts in the paranormal community. Mark and Debby Constantino are two EVP specialists based out of Reno. They are a husband-and-wife team of paranormal investigators who get EVP almost everywhere they go. They've become a magnet for spirit activity. They have captured literally thousands of spirit voices and have helped us get better at recording our own EVP. Because we've also become friends, we also find ways to mess with those guys.

On a flight one day, Billy Tolley, the *Ghost Adventures* evidence reviewer who comes with us on most of our investigations, took a photo of me sitting in my seat on the airplane. He used a ghost capture app for the iPhone to plant a semitransparent ghostly figure in the empty seat next to me. I sent it to Mark and Debby and told them our plane was haunted. It was hokey enough that they knew it was a fake, but we all had a good laugh.

The fact that people were turning to me with their evidence meant we were making a connection with people. When we were out filming season one, we were traveling all over, just the three of us. We didn't like being cooped up in motel rooms on the first two nights of filming, so we'd always go out, meet up with the locals, and see what's up. I love socializing in new places, and we were starting to find that wherever we went, people were recognizing us from the documentary that was airing so often on SciFi. And every one of them had a story to tell. Everybody likes to make that connection with another person.

I'll always take the time to talk to fans when we're traveling. Not only do I enjoy the exchange, I also get to hear firsthand what parts of the show resonate with them. Most often, it's the lockdown. Viewers like to see the actual investigation and the evidence we turn up.

QUESTIONS FANS ASK

What is your favorite piece of ghost hunting equipment?

I like my digital audio recorder. I feel like I have a connection to speak with spirits on the other side, and this is the easiest way for us to do that.

Going out on the town on one of the nights was pretty much our only downtime on the shoots, though. On the third night, we'd go in for the lockdown, and then head home after that.

Then it was right to analysis and editing, which would keep Zak and me holed up in one room together again until we were done.

That process alone was nerve-racking. What if they lost the tapes? We'd be screwed! I had to mail them everything—the hard drives, the master tapes. I was still new to Final Cut, so it was taking longer than I would have liked. Plus, the rendering time to get the footage loaded onto the computer was killing me. Even when I'd finally got the hang of the new software and the editing process in general, I still couldn't believe how much time was being wasted waiting for the tapes to render.

We decided the simplest solution would be to compress the footage from high definition to standard definition for our edit, and then when we sent it to the production company in New York they could recapture it in HD. It was still time-consuming, but it was our best option, and also a learning experience. It was my first time working in real television, and I was figuring out how to make it all work. I was pretty damn proud of that.

All the stress and long hours started to take a toll on our lives outside the show, and with our family and friends. I tried as hard as I could to keep some semblance of a normal relationship with Veronique, but it wasn't easy. I give her a lot of props for all her patience. I'd be on the road, then get home, and still she wouldn't see me all day and sometimes all night. My body paid a price for it too.

In fact, I got so damn skinny filming season one that I had to do something about it. I was on the road, which is a strain in itself, but then I wasn't working out or eating properly. Even when I wasn't traveling or spending all night investigating, I spent every other moment chained to an editing suite. It was hell on my body. One night I came home and Veronique just stared at me. "Wow—you're so skinny," she said. "You're way too skinny." I never would have thought filming a television show would be that tough on my health.

When we wrapped up the first season, my cousin Justin came to live with me for a bit. He's really smart about things like personal training—he's been ripped since high school, back when he played football. He can lift twice his body weight. He's one of those dudes that you just don't want to fuck with. While he was staying with me, we were working on things like scripts and concepts for other TV shows, but we also worked out quite a bit. He got me ripped, and I went from being a scrawny 175 pounds to being 205 and all muscle. I started drinking protein shakes, and I was jacked. Justin had me kicking ass in the gym, which made me feel better about myself.

QUESTIONS FANS ASK

What does it feel like to be possessed? Do you still have some control over your thoughts and actions?

I wouldn't describe my experience as having been possessed. It's more that a dark energy has taken over my own body and mind. I do have control, but that is the dangerous part of losing sight of your own energy.

It was actually Aaron who noticed first. He started making some stupid comments to me, like, "I kind of liked skinny Nick a little bit better. Zak's supposed to be the ripped one, I'm the overweight one, and you're the skinny one!"

Of course, it's funny now, because Aaron started eating right and he lost a ton of weight himself. Now Zak, he took it a little differently. Zak's a competitive guy, and he's always making everything into a competition. I'm competitive too—it's always been in my nature and I hate to lose. Whether it was swimming, or basketball, or whatever, I've always had to win. I wasn't looking to compete with Zak when it came to our bodies, but he kind of took it that way.

Zak and I were working out together one time at a shoot. We were in a hospital because it was the only place around that had a gym. I'd been keeping on top of my workout plan, eating right, keeping my weight up, all that stuff. And as we were working out, Zak looked at me and said, "Dude, how can you just go from 175 to 205? There's no way you can do that."

I knew where he was going with it, and I didn't like it. I asked him what he was getting at.

He eventually laid off me, but he still tried to lift more than me that day.

It happens all the time, though, these little competitions. Maybe it's just part of the male bonding. You know that game in some bars where you put in a dollar and punch the machine as hard as you can to try to get the highest score? Yeah, we do that anytime we're out together and find one of those machines—thank God there aren't many of those around anymore.

I took tae kwon do as a kid. My dad got me into it when I was five or six, and I followed it all the way through and earned my black belt. He got me into it because he knew it would help me stay in control of my emotions, but also if I got in a fight, at least I'd know how to defend myself. I continued it all the way through college at UNLV, even shooting some tae kwon do videos with one of my professors. It was a big part of my life growing up.

So if there's one thing I know, it's how to throw a punch—and how to focus all my strength and power into my fist as I'm throwing it. I would punch the stupid machine as hard as I could, scoring 900 or something. When Zak took his turn, he didn't score as high as me. He just kept feeding money into the machine until he beat my number. I ended up with bloody knuckles after missing and punching a hole in the wall on one of my turns. It's funny how competitive we can get with each other.

Punching a wall offers an ironic lesson: If you're going to work in the television production business, you need to be able to tolerate some pain. Sometimes you have to punch; sometimes you have to negotiate. You have to remind yourself that no matter how many disagreements, at the end of the day we all want the same thing: a kick-ass show.

Different locations and episodes have stuck with viewers for different reasons. One location that makes many fans' top five lists is Bobby Mackey's Music World in Wilder, Kentucky. I'd been dying to go to this place for years, and I'd mentioned it to Zak and Aaron as a possible future investigation just as we were finishing our documentary. As soon as we got the green light on the series, Bobby Mackey's made our season one short list right away.

Bobby Mackey's is a former slaughterhouse with connections to cult activity, suicide, and heartbreak. When you put all that together in one place, it will draw in negative energy and spirits.

ABOUT BOBBY MACKEY'S MUSIC WORLD

Today, Bobby Mackey's Music World is a popular nightclub full of song, dancing, and good times. The cheerful setting, however, also holds something more sinister. Some have claimed the building's basement holds the gateway to hell itself—in an abandoned well discovered in the bowels of the building.

Many cultures have long associated water with paranormal activity. Some believe that spirits can't cross flowing waters. So perhaps it is the rare northern-running current of the Licking River that keeps the dark forces trapped inside the building.

The roadhouse that sits at 44 Licking Pike has a bloody history and a shady past. On this site in 1850, a large slaughterhouse and meatpacking facility were constructed that would serve northwestern Kentucky and nearby Cincinnati, Ohio.

In the lowest part of the building sat a well to hold the unused blood, guts, and waste from the slaughtered animals. This was long before the days of electricity and refrigeration. On warm days the area around the building would reek of death.

The slaughterhouse closed in the 1890s and then sat empty, but not unused, according to many legends. Some researchers have speculated that satanic cult activity took place in the building around the well. Animals, and possibly humans, were slaughtered here for ritualistic purposes during secret meetings.

In 1896, the murder of twenty-two-year-old Pearl Bryan, a small-town girl from Greencastle, Indiana, made all the headlines in the region. Pearl's body was discovered in a field less

(Continued)

than two miles from the slaughterhouse, but her corpse was discovered headless.

Pearl was pregnant, so her boyfriend, Scott Jackson, a student at the Ohio College of Dental Surgery, urged her to come to Cincinnati, where he could arrange an abortion for her. Jackson and his roommate, Alonzo Walling, attempted the abortion themselves, but something went horribly wrong. To cover their tracks, they brought Pearl's body out to an empty field and cut off her head so she couldn't be identified. They might have gotten away with the cover-up, but they'd left Pearl's shoes on her feet. Shoes made especially for her in her hometown of Greencastle.

Pearl's severed head was never discovered, though some have speculated that Jackson had ties to the satanic cult that held rituals in the old slaughterhouse. Some believe the head made its way to the basement of the building to be used for dark incantations.

Scott Jackson and Alonzo Walling were both sentenced to the gallows. Police investigators pleaded with the men to disclose where they'd hidden the severed head, but the men maintained their innocence. They were executed on March 21, 1897.

The slaughterhouse was razed in the early part of the twentieth century. The lot sat empty until the 1920s, when the property was born again with a new building that served as a casino, nightclub, and eventual speakeasy during Prohibition.

When Prohibition ended in 1933, E. A. "Buck" Brady bought the building and called it the Primrose. After more than a decade of successful operations, his casino caught the attention of Cincinnati mobsters who tried to muscle their way into the operation. When Brady refused to sell, the violence escalated with fighting and threats to customers in the parking lot, until 1946, when Buck drew a gun on a local mobster named Albert "Red" Masterson. Soon after, Brady was charged with attempted murder and left the casino business.

Then, in the 1950s, the building reopened as a nightclub called the Latin Quarter. It was during this time that the club's most prominent ghostly figure traces its roots. It's the classic story of forbidden love. Johanna, the daughter of the nightclub's owner, fell in love with a singer who performed there. She got pregnant and intended to run off with the young singer. Her father forbade the romance, however, and used his criminal connections to have the singer killed. When Johanna discovered her lover had been murdered, she attempted to poison her father, then took her own life in the basement of the building.

The dark past of 44 Licking Pike came to an abrupt end in 1978, when a series of fatal shootings at the rough-and-tumble nightclub forced local authorities to close the establishment.

Later that same year, a young country singer named Bobby Mackey bought the building and turned it into the music hall and tavern that still stands today. Paranormal phenomena have been present since day one. Though Bobby himself is skeptical, he'll admit that he doesn't doubt the words of many eyewitnesses over the years who have experienced something powerful and unexplained in the building.

Nightclub employees, local police officers, and even patrons all have accounts of being shoved by unseen forces, witnessing specters walking throughout the building, and even cases of demonic possession. Though clergy and psychics have tried to help, there's a dark force that still lingers inside.

Legends are curious things. They're created by people, but there's always some root to them based in fact. We don't know for sure about the cult activity, we don't know if there's a connection between Pearl Bryan's missing head and the building, but we *do* know the place is haunted. We spoke to the witnesses who had been pushed down the stairs. We saw the video footage of the exorcism attempt on Carl Lawson, a former employee and caretaker of the building who actually lived in an apartment upstairs from the bar for several years. The reasons for the haunting may be in dispute, but the fact that it's an active dark place is not.

As soon as I walked in there, I felt on edge. This was the second location we filmed, though it was the first to air. The reason for the switch was because of all the insane activity that happened. This place got personal really fast.

Though we were still new at *Ghost Adventures*, I had been on enough paranormal investigations to know that you can sit for hours with nothing happening. Bobby Mackey's wasn't like that. This place was active the entire night. I was wiped out by the end just trying to keep up with everything.

Even when I was taking a short break something happened. We knew from talking to witnesses that people had been assaulted in the men's room in previous years, but you don't think about that when you have to piss, you know? As I walked into the bathroom, suddenly I heard a loud bang that sent me running out. When we went back in with cameras, it happened again. My heart was racing the entire night. It's so rare that things happen in the same spot just as you're watching—that's somehow more frightening than experiencing the paranormal in a place you don't expect.

After the strange banging sound in the bathroom, Zak started provoking just outside the men's room. He yelled at whatever entity might be listening when he suddenly felt a burning sensation down his back. When he lifted his shirt, we could see three scratch marks! *Holy shit* was the only thing I could think at this point. Banging noises and seeing shadows are passive. It happens in the building, you know? Getting scratched is a physical assault. It occurred to me for the first time that what we were doing might put me in danger. It was incredible enough that we'd already captured the banging and the scratches on camera. But there was more to come.

Down by the old well, we caught a shadow figure on camera. You have to understand that any one of these events is a once-in-a-lifetime capture for a paranormal investigator. We had it all happen on the same night.

After we were done with the shoot, Aaron said something sinister followed him home. To this day he won't go into much detail because it's so deeply personal. But he later admitted on camera that he believes whatever it was broke up his marriage.

The stuff we captured was so amazing that we called the network and told them they had to move that episode up to being the series premiere.

And the network did it too, which was no small feat. The first episode had to be scheduled months in advance, because of all the programming involved, the release of show information, the promotion and commercials to publicize the series, and everything like that. So it really meant a lot that the Travel Channel was willing to stick their necks out like that and move up the Mackey's episode. It meant they put their trust in us.

We made it through filming that first season, but that's not to say there weren't times when I felt like I'd had enough. In fact, the seventh episode of that season, at a mental hospital in New Jersey, was when I first reached my breaking point. Filming there freaked me out. Thousands of people had died at that old place over the years, and it was very creepy.

QUESTIONS FANS ASK

How do you avoid bumping into things in complete darkness?

I do bump into things . . . often! I'll show you the scars and bruises sometime. One problem with showing us walking into stuff on the show is that it will make you laugh and break the mood of the location and moment. So fortunately—or unfortunately if you're the kind of person that likes to see us get hurt—those moments end up on the cutting room floor.

Getting into this location to film and investigate was a trick. We had to agree not to name the location in the episode because the town was afraid that tons of people would come there after seeing it on *Ghost Adventures* and break in at night. That's a legit concern. The more popular our show has become, the more people want to go where we've gone and become part of the legend.

I can tell you now that the place was Essex County Hospital. Of course, within minutes of the episode airing, some people recognized where we were and posted the name online.

ABOUT ESSEX COUNTY HOSPITAL

Built in the late 1800s, Essex County Hospital and the surrounding buildings were constructed on hundreds of acres.
The site was intended to be self-sufficient—the facility grew
its own food, produced electricity, and even had its own fire
department. The objective was not to financially burden the
surrounding community while helping the patients live a
somewhat normal life away from the torment and nightmares
that waited for them inside their own minds.

In the early part of the twentieth century, psychology was
still in its infancy. Practices that we'd consider barbaric today
were commonplace in treating the mentally disturbed. Shock
therapy, ice water baths, and even lobotomies were just some
of the techniques used on psychiatric patients. Sometimes
the treatments were worse than the affliction—driving some
further into madness, and others to murder and suicide.

Psychiatric patients were often the unwanted of society. In
some cases, the mentally disabled were abandoned by their
families, leaving large institutions as their only hope for their
basic needs. But life inside could be grueling, to say the least.

The hospital suffered a major catastrophe in the winter of
1917, when the hospital's heating plant broke down. For weeks
patients went without heat, and twenty-four people died
within twenty days, some freezing to death in their beds.
Though the hospital brought in oil-burning stoves to offer
some relief from the cold, the stoves were forbidden in the

(Continued)

criminally insane building because the administration feared the patients might use the oil to set fires.

During the Great Depression, thousands of Americans were homeless and hungry. People were having themselves committed to institutions like this one because it meant a roof over their heads, but soon these facilities became dangerously overcrowded. Hospital staff simply could not care for so many people, and the overall population suffered.

Working at the hospital was a challenge even under normal conditions. The screams, unnatural laughs, and painful moans of the patients could eat away at even the most hardened orderly's nerves. Attempts at escape, violence among the residents, and the occasional patient abuse by staff pushed to the brink have left a permanent mark on this facility.

During the 1970s, funding for large psychiatric institutions dwindled, leaving many struggling to provide basic care. Advances in medication meant that some people could move out of institutions and back into society, but some were simply turned out onto the street, where they had to fend for themselves.

As funding and patient population declined, Essex County buildings were shut down and left to rot. Slowly the paint peeled away and the surrounding forest grew closer, threatening to swallow the land and reclaim it. Several years ago the few remaining active buildings shut their doors for good, leaving the massive complex to decay into obscurity and legend.

For years, stories have circulated about disembodied voices echoing through the empty hallways. The firehouse is said to be haunted by a former fireman who died after a tragic fall within the building. In some of the patient wards, even darker forces have been reported. The phantom cries of tormented patients seem to be a residual haunting—a kind of psychic recording that plays over and over.

Other forces are both interactive and dark. Black shadows have been seen lurking in the buildings and in the network of underground tunnels. Those who have ventured into the patient wards have reported a threatening, unwelcome feeling—these witnesses ran away and didn't catch their breath until they were safely out of the building.

The New Jersey hospital was an intense place. It was dirty and dusty—the first time we had to use air masks—and the activity seemed to be everywhere. Some viewers found the breathing masks distracting; some even called us pussies. But seriously, when you spend days in dangerous asbestos-filled locations that are closed off to the public, your lungs fill up with that crap. You should see some of the liability waivers we've had to sign to get into old buildings like Essex County Hospital. I'm not a lawyer, but let me quickly sum up the gist of what these waivers say: "There's a ton of bad shit in this building—bad shit to breathe in, bad places to step, and weak structures. There's a great chance you're going to get hurt, sick, and maybe even die. You agree not to sue us for anything, ever. Have a great time! Sign here: _____ "

I'm in no rush to become a ghost myself, so occasionally I'm going to wear an air mask on the show.

When you get into a location where very few have gone before, it's like whatever is inside finds you immediately because human activity is so rare.

This investigation wiped me out. Being a self-sufficient facility meant Essex had its own morgue. This was the first time I would get locked inside one of these things. Even though I've been a daredevil since I was a kid, this was something different for me. I went inside with my camera and audio recorder, and Zak locked me in. You know what? For the first few minutes it wasn't a big deal. I could handle it fine. But the minutes stretched longer and longer and soon the silence was deafening. That tight space starts to mess with your mind. Now I'm hearing things—I know the sounds were in my head because my audio recorder didn't pick them up. I'm sweating in there . . . I start to imagine, maybe even channel what it's like to be a corpse inside that unforgiving box.

Then I hear the sound of shuffling feet outside the morgue door when Zak and Aaron are nowhere near me. I can hear something pushing against the metal door of the locker. Now I'm starting to sweat. My heart is racing. Later I would see from the stationary camera we'd aimed at the body locker I was in that there was a force moving the door. Inside the box I'm trying to keep cool enough to record an EVP session. I captured only one spirit voice there. It said, "Die."

Panic is starting to set in; then I see a glowing face down by my feet and I lose it. I start kicking against the door. I can only think about getting the hell out of that box right now! Zak hears the pounding and screaming and finally runs in to let me out. That experience was some of the most intense fear I've ever experienced.

Once I got home, those bad feelings got worse. The location may have played some role in what I was going through, but there was much more. I edited that episode by myself, and when I got about halfway through I just felt like I couldn't do it anymore. I was exhausted. I never would have guessed that I'd be working on a television show and be this overwhelmed. I thought there would be help with this stuff, that we'd have a support staff. The reality is we didn't have a huge budget, so we all had to pull a lot of weight. And given that this was the seventh out of eight episodes in the first season, I wasn't sure I could go on. I was staring at the computer doing nothing. Just staring straight ahead for minutes at a time. I felt like I had no life—nothing but work. Every muscle in my body wanted to get up, walk away, and turn off the lights behind me.

And that was just what I did. I walked away and went outside for some air. Probably the only thing that made me turn around and get back to the edit was the simple fact that I'm not a quitter. I was going to finish this fucker, and do the next episode. After that, I could rest and rethink everything. I became singularly focused to get this and the next episode done. My background in sports helped me a lot. I had flashes of those UNLV soccer tryouts where I'd physically pushed myself past the breaking point. Being a competitor has taught me that my limits are almost always in my mind—they can be overcome.

We were almost finished filming the first season when the first episode premiered. All those hours of work, the arguments, the amazing moments, the effort of the entire production team was about to come together. Friday, October 17, 2008—a day I'll never forget. It was the best feeling in the world, seeing promos all day long on the Travel Channel, and then, as nine p.m. was drawing near, I was giddy inside. It was like watching the original documentary on the SciFi Channel . . . only times a hundred. We had little parties and get-togethers for the new episodes as they premiered, and I started to realize that we really did have something great. It was unique, it was gritty, it was real, and I felt like we were making our mark both as filmmakers and as paranormal investigators.

QUESTIONS FANS ASK

What has been your favorite place to investigate?

Virginia City, Nevada. Hands down. That town keeps calling me back. I feel like I have a connection with the Washoe Club. Each time I go to Virginia City I learn something new, I find some new haunt. I'll never get tired of that place.

What I wasn't prepared for was the level of fame that came as a result. I was used to getting recognized at paranormal events or asked to critique evidence because of the documentary, but this was a whole new level of exposure. After four or five episodes, I was starting to get recognized in public.

Let me say this: our fans rock. They are amazing, they're dedicated, and we love them as much as they love us. But it's still a little jarring when you're standing at the airport in Manchester, New Hampshire—one of the tiniest airports around—and you're getting recognized. When people are driving by in a car and start screaming "Ghost Adventures! Ghost Adventures!" out the window, it's pretty bizarre. But at the same time it's really cool. This thing that had started as a dream in my apartment was now a hit television show.

But I also know that fame will never change who I am. I always stick to my roots, where I came from and who I am. I'll never say no to anybody or act like I'm too big for them. I'll take a picture with anyone who asks, I'll sign an autograph, because there are already too many egos in the television industry. Me, I'm just a human being like anybody else, and this is my job.

Though I did change in certain ways. I watched myself on the episodes and wanted to be better. I went from being the guy who had told Zak that I just wanted to be behind the camera, not in front of it, to being the guy who started editing myself because I felt too much of what I said sounded stupid or lame. I became conscious of what my image was going to be to the public, and started to care more about how I came out looking from this whole experience. I thought about the clothes I was wearing, what I said, and how I said it. That may sound like a compromise from keeping it raw and real, but I look at it more as wanting to put some polish on what I was already doing. If I was going to be successful at taking the audience into a haunted location with me, I didn't want any distractions. So I took the time to think about what to say and what to wear.

We improved in front of the camera pretty quickly. We filmed a lot of videos for the Travel Channel's Web site in which we recounted some of our experiences at a location, and those were good because it was just us and the camera. We also started doing other specials, like "Best Evidence" and "Scariest Moments." Those helped me gain confidence too.

I learned that if you want to get better on camera you need to film yourself and watch yourself in an objective way. You'll see your flaws pretty quickly—we all have them. We might slouch a little bit, or use too many "ums" when we talk, and that stuff can be fixed.

Life as a television personality is different from being some young guy in a documentary. You even start to look at yourself differently. For one thing, I looked back at the documentary and cringed at the shorts and stupid shirt I was wearing. *I wore that?* I wondered. *Couldn't I have worn some cool jeans or a cool shirt or something?*

Hey, I said I didn't change who I was as a person. That doesn't mean I couldn't get a better sense of style.

Besides, we must have done something right. Before the Travel Channel had aired all eight episodes in our first season, they had already decided to sign us for season two! This little documentary and now series was turning into a hit.

My nose has a cut on it from being adventurous.

The childhood doll my aunt used to freak me out when I was five.

Me, age eighteen, and Veronique, age seventeen, at our junior prom on the Spirit of Boston boat.

The Washoe Club exterior, Virginia City, Nevada. An extremely scary location for me personally and where we captured a full-body apparition on a static night vision camera I set up in the ballroom. Where it all started for us during the documentary.

Getting ready to enter the sewer drain and look for the entrance to Bobby Mackey's well to the basement.

Entering the sewer drain in search of the passageway to Bobby Mackey's well in the basement of the building.

Me wearing a hospital air mask at Essex County Hospital because the air quality was so poor. Deep underground in the tunnel systems.

Moon River Brewery, top floor. This location gave me a rude awakening on dangerous energies that can overtake one's body and mind. A very scary location!

I was dared to climb a wall on a small street in Venice, Italy. I accepted the dare and kept climbing. I loved Venice.

The Trans-Allegheny Lunatic Asylum. This was where the seven-hour live episode in the fifth season took place.

Linda Vista Hospital. This is where I had the most haunting ghost experience of my life.

I saw the woman spirit right here, at Linda Vista Hospital, in front of this machine.

Here I am dressed up at Gettysburg. I loved becoming part of the past through these clothes and prop guns. It helped me realize what these people went through in this period of their life.

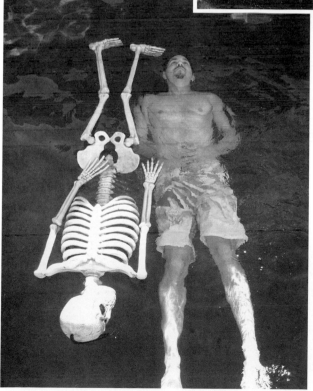

Hanging out in Aaron's pool with my skeleton friend.

Here's what makes it all worthwhile: my family. My wife, Veronique, and daughter, Annabelle, came to visit me after I had finished filming the Winchester Mystery House episode in San Jose, California. We are relaxing at Malibu Beach!

Me, having fun in the Valley of Fire. Veronique and I drove outside Las Vegas to take a day trip and explore nature.

CHAPTER 10

WHAT'S A GHOST AND HOW DO WE FIND ONE?

The more you investigate the paranormal, the more you start to get a feel for what works and what doesn't. Each location is different, so what works at Bobby Mackey's Music World may not work on Poveglia Island.

One lesson *Ghost Adventures* has taught me is that this stuff is real, and it's a lot more prevalent than I'd previously thought. I've picked up a lot of ideas on how to investigate and how to get results from each location. Does it work every time? No. I've had plenty of misses, but I've also had a lot of successes in gathering profound evidence of spirit contact.

Going to so many haunted places has caused me to think about what might be out there and why our equipment helps us make contact.

When I was a kid, I thought a ghost was some apparition that comes into our world to scare us. That's what ghost stories taught me, and it's the theme that Hollywood ran with. But now I realize an apparition is only one version of the ghost experience. It's also the most rare.

Here's an experiment you can try right now: Think of a friend from your childhood. Go ahead—close your eyes and envision that friend. You can actually see that person. Your memory fired some electrochemical impulses in your brain that allowed you to visualize your friend. Energy made that happen.

Energy can't be created or destroyed; it can only change forms—that's a law of physics. *Not* a theory of physics—a *law*. It's called the law of conservation of energy. It means that if you take an isolated system, such as a person, the energy contained in that person can't be destroyed. It can change forms from chemical energy—like the signals that travel down your nerve pathways—into kinetic energy, the energy required to move your arm, for example, but the energy is always there.

This law makes sense to me. It means that when we die, our energy must go somewhere. The flesh and bones—the empty vessel—is left behind, but the energy survives.

Every time we remember someone who has passed on, we are using an electrical impulse in our brain to call up that person's image. That memory and image gives you a connection to that person. This is why so many people have visitation experiences involving their deceased loved ones.

The ghost experience isn't just seeing an apparition. People can sense ghosts, like the way you can tell when someone walks into the room behind you. People can smell ghosts—I can't tell you how many times witnesses have reported smelling perfume or a cigar when no source can be found. Smell is closely related to memory, so that scent may call up something specific in the case of a deceased loved one. People hear ghosts—sometimes we hear disembodied voices in a location. And then, of course, there's actually seeing something. The ghost experience involves our senses. There's no way around it.

So if spirits are energy, and if we need our senses to experience them, then we have a lot of equipment available that can be adapted to help us validate what we're experiencing in a haunted location.

QUESTIONS FANS ASK

How can you tell the difference between a paranormal orb in a photo and something natural like dust or moisture?

Orbs are a controversial topic in the paranormal. Most of the orbs you see in photographs are just halos around dust or moisture. Sometimes what you're seeing is lens flare—light reflecting and refracting off the numerous lenses inside a camera. *But* there are those balls of light that glow—they produce light. Those are interesting and very rare. If the orb is producing its own light and even illuminating the area around it, it's not just dust or drops of moisture.

It's been a learning curve—we're always experimenting with this stuff—but we've seen that our gear is clearly a factor in connecting us to what we experience out there.

Let me start with the basics. Ouija boards. There's no item in the paranormal discussion that's more controversial. The Ouija board is actually a brand name—a trademark that belongs to Hasbro. It's kind of like how people call a tissue a Kleenex or a photocopier a Xerox machine. The generic term is a "talking board" or "spirit board," for any device with letters and numbers on it and some kind of pointer, or planchette, used to spell out messages. The Ouija board came around in 1891 and has been the most commercially successful talking board ever.

Ouija was first manufactured by the Kennard Novelty Company in Baltimore, Maryland. In 1891, five men invested thirty thousand dollars to mass-produce a new kind of board game. Their bet paid off. In 1967, this "game" outsold Monopoly. There is nothing inherently evil about cardboard and plastic. But like anything else, it's all in how you use it.

I understand the talking board. If I were turned into a spirit right now, I could use one of these devices. I mean, I know how to spell, and I can move the pointer around, so I could get a message across. The reason this board is so controversial is because it has a stigma attached to it. That stigma dates back only to the 1970s, when the book and then movie *The Exorcist* came out. There's a brief scene in the movie where a young girl named Regan MacNeil (played by Linda Blair) uses a Ouija board in her house by herself as she communicates with an entity she calls "Captain Howdy."

Ever since the 1970s many paranormal investigators have pointed to this movie as an example of why you shouldn't use Ouija boards. These critics will say you shouldn't use them because you don't know what could be coming through on the other side. Here's the thing: we never know what's on the other side—whether we use a Ouija board, an EMF meter, an Ovilus, or any other method. We're invoking the spirit to come to us and communicate. Each method has its risks. If you feel the practice is dangerous, that's fine—I understand. But in that case, it's probably best for you to stay away from paranormal investigation entirely. I also understand those people who say they get better results using one method over another—that's fair. What I don't understand is calling one method a doorway to evil and others safe based entirely on hearsay and rumor. The Ouija board's reputation, for one, has a powerful effect on people. Some people are afraid to use it, and that fear doesn't serve you in the paranormal. Having confidence in yourself and control of your thoughts and emotions does.

In the original documentary, we used a Ouija board in the Miner's Lodge of the Gold Hill Hotel in Virginia City. You see it briefly in the documentary, but that's about it. In reality, filming people using a Ouija board isn't very compelling. Even if the messages are profound, they still come out one letter at a time.

Back to spirit contact: I also understand how we could use an EMF meter—an electronic device used to measure electromagnetic activity in the area—such as a KII or Mel meter to communicate. Electromagnetic activity is happening all around us all the time. If you took one of these meters and held it near your television while it was turned on, the meter would spike because your TV radiates energy due to the electricity and wiring inside. If a spirit gets close to an EMF meter and it lights up, you could easily use this to establish communication with the spirit. For example, ask it to touch the device once for yes and twice for no. I get all that.

The thing with EMF meters, though, is that many natural causes can set them off. We live on a big magnet called Earth, after all, so when these devices go off, we need to validate that it's due to more than random chance. If I ask a question and get a reaction from an EMF meter or one of our pods, I ask an immediate follow-up like: "Make it flash twice now." If the device responds to my specific commands, then I know I'm communicating with something intelligent as opposed to a random event.

QUESTIONS FANS ASK

Do you think ghosts are really with us all the time, rather than fleeting presences? The more we learn about physics, the more it sounds like this may be the case.

That's definitely possible. One theory is that there are many different dimensions all around us, maybe even alternate universes. Quantum physics suggests that every choice that each individual makes creates an alternate universe where a different choice was made. I know it sounds mind-blowing, but here's a simple example: You walk down an alleyway. You get to the end and can turn left or right. If you decide to go left, then there's a whole other universe that exists than had you decided to turn right. Billions of people making millions of choices each day and you have an infinite number of dimensions.

One theory is that these dimensions stack up next to each other like sheets of paper. Sometimes something like a cosmic quake erupts and two points on the sheet of paper touch—each dimension sees the other for a brief period of time. Seeing a person from a different time period in the environment would definitely look like a ghost!

My favorite method for spirit communication is still the audio recorder. Like the Ouija board or EMF meter, this method is also clear to me: I'm asking the spirits to get close to the microphone and speak as loud as they can. EVP, or electronic voice phenomena, isn't recorded as audio. It's imprinted directly onto the magnetic tape or circuit. The idea of EVP goes back at least a century, to when ethnologist Waldemar Bogoras took his recording equipment to Siberia to record a spirit conjuring ritual of the Chukchi tribe. In the recording you can hear a voice tweak out and overpower the audio equipment, though the voice of the shaman performing the ritual remains constant. EVP really took off in the late 1950s when a Swedish painter and musician named Friedrich Jürgenson took his audio recorder out into the woods to record the sounds of nature. On the playback, he heard voices. From there the equipment has evolved from reel-to-reel recorders to tape recorders, then to digital recorders and so on, but the idea has always been the same: you ask a question and get a response on the recorder even though you haven't heard the voice with your ears. It's amazing when it happens. To those who are skeptical, I invite you to try it for yourself.

EVP is the most powerful evidence we can offer. Though I've captured hundreds of EVP readings by now, each one still blows me away.

When it comes to more complicated devices like the Ovilus, PX, or Spirit Box/Shack Hack (devices that quickly cycle through radio waves allowing spirits to manipulate the sounds into words and sentences), I don't have all the answers on how these things work. I've included a section at the end of this book on paranormal investigation equipment (see page 239), where I talk to the people who invented these things so you can hear about the technology behind these things straight from the horse's mouth. But even the inventors stop short of telling you *why* it works. All I can say is it's worth experimenting, because sometimes you'll get amazing results.

For example, we were investigating a historic home called Rocky Point Manor in Harrodsburg, Kentucky, in season five. This old home saw some serious shit during the Civil War. After the Battle of Perryville on October 8, 1862, Confederate forces retreated. Both Union and Confederate soldiers took over any building they encountered to convert into a field hospital. Anything you had in your house, from food to linens to furniture, was seized. The timing couldn't have been worse. It was October, so many families had stocked up on supplies for the winter, and now they had nothing.

Likewise, Rocky Point Manor had become a field hospital. Many soldiers lost their limbs and some lost their lives. We found all kinds of artifacts in the dirt-floor basement, from bones to belt buckles.

During this investigation, I was out in the Perryville battlefields with my PX device—a kind of EMF meter with a built-in audio dictionary. The PX takes readings of the electromagnetic field and runs it through software to determine a number. That number corresponds with a word in the dictionary. We believe spirits can use this device to communicate with us. For two hours we were out there and this thing didn't speak up once—that in itself is rare, as usually the PX won't go more than a few minutes before it says something. So we headed over to Rocky Point Manor and set up an experiment where we had cameras on a room with lines back to monitors at a base. We took turns going in. Aaron went in and the PX said nothing. I was next. Just as I was about to leave, I put my hand on the doorknob and the PX said, "Close"—as in, close the door. Okay, fine, could be a hell of a coincidence. So now we all got quiet and I asked, "Why?" and then the PX says, "Nick." So now I'm thinking this isn't just a chance. I can't tell you how the spirits manipulated the circuits, but something happened to spit those two words out at that exact moment. But that wasn't the end of it. After I walked out into the hallway, it said, "Enemy." Considering this was a field hospital, that word had significance. At the same time it said the word "enemy," I felt an electric charge run through my body.

The equipment is great because it can validate your experience. The best judge, however, is you, the living person. When you feel that tingle, the hair stand up on the back of your neck, you might be in the presence of something.

So we have all this gear, but how do we make sure we're making the best use of it when we bring it to a haunted location? First, you have to know the history of a place before you go in. You need to know what took place there, who lived there, and how they died. When you know those things, you'll ask the right questions and get better results. It makes me crazy when investigators want to go into a location without doing their research first—that's just lazy. The history is the stage these ghosts stand on. Without the history, we're guessing, and that's not the way to do a paranormal investigation.

By interviewing people from the location ahead of time, we already have a sense about what the most active parts of the building might be. That doesn't mean we'll ignore the other rooms, but it does mean we think twice about where to set up our static cameras.

During the investigation, we want to be thorough. During setup, I'll often walk around with an EMF meter to see where the electromagnetic forces spike around the building. This doesn't mean ghosts necessarily—it could also mean there are electric wires running through the wall. If I know where those high-EMF areas are, I can rule out false positives when they occur.

Though each place needs a different investigation plan, in general we want to walk through the entire location to see what we feel and what our equipment picks up. This is part of the investigation you rarely see on the show, because it's the least exciting part of the lockdown. When you do see parts of this process, it's because something has happened during the setup. Sometimes things start happening almost as soon as we enter a building. The Riddle House in West Palm Beach, Florida, was one of those locations. We had just shut the door when we heard a banging noise. Some places seem like they're waiting for us.

Earlier I said that there are advantages to investigating in a group because you have other people around to validate your findings. That's true. But if you've seen *Ghost Adventures*, you know there are plenty of times when we split up and go solo. There are a couple reasons for that. First, it could be that the spirit entities are intimidated by the group and may be more likely to make contact with just one of us. The other reason is fear.

When you're afraid, your senses are heightened and you're more open to whatever else might be in the environment. If you're alone and scared, you're sharper. Sometimes it's the only way to have a personal paranormal experience.

It's amazing how much braver you get with even one other person there. I recall hosting an event at the Ohio State Reformatory in Mansfield, Ohio. We had filmed an episode of *Ghost Adventures* at this place in our second season—it turned out to be one of our most popular episodes. The place is insanely active all over.

During events like this, we lead groups that can be as large as twenty-five to thirty people. I remember talking to one girl who said she wasn't scared at all—this place didn't frighten her. Really? We were in a giant building. It was dark. The paint was peeling, there were strange breezes and sounds all around us, and six stories of rusted cages used for the prisoners. But she was in a group.

"Okay," I told her. I moved her to the center of the cell block and told her to start walking to the far wall. There was very little light, but just enough to see where you were walking. She was fine for a few steps, but soon it got darker and she couldn't hear or see us anymore. I heard her footsteps fading in the distance as she was walking alone past dark prison cells. Those old doors were wide-open. Out of the corner of your eye it looked like someone was always ready to jump out. A few seconds later I heard her yelp and the distinct sound of her running footsteps coming our way.

"Oh, shit! I saw something," she said as she tried to catch her breath.

The fear had made her more sensitive and open. It's a natural physiological response that dates back to our early human ancestors who had to pay close attention to their environment or else would be eaten by animals or attacked by enemies fighting for the limited resources of the land.

Once we've completed the initial survey or sweep of the location, we head to the hot spots—those areas where witnesses have reported strange things happening. We might set up our static X-cams or do some experiments to see what happens. This is why knowing the history is critical. You *will* get better results by making specific remarks and asking pointed questions, as opposed to saying, "Hello? Anybody there?"

In many cases we use provocation to stir things up, which is one of the most controversial aspects of what we do. We call out the entities that might be there. We charge the environment with our own energy. We invite physical contact.

It's like preparing for a fight. We're showing we're not afraid. "Go ahead—do something to me!" We're ready to stand up to these things. No fear. Fear invites these entities inside of you and gives them room to get comfortable. By a show of force, we're protecting ourselves. But no, it doesn't always work. Sometimes these things push back.

Nor do we use provocation every time. If we're dealing with spirits who did no harm in life, then we might take a different approach. But I'm always pushing for spirit contact, whether it's by a show of force or by a trigger object.

Trigger objects are really old-school ghost hunting. You put out an item that might have some meaning to the spirit there and see if they react. On *Ghost Adventures* we've used toys, shots of booze, and many other effects to try to get a response. We're all drawn to objects in some way—people love their jewelry or their liquor, or a child might be comforted by a familiar toy. So it's natural that they'd want to reach out and interact with one of these objects from the other side.

On a few investigations we've brought in psychics. In season two, we used Chris Fleming for our live episode at Trans-Allegheny Lunatic Asylum in Weston, West Virginia. We also brought in psychics for the Riddle House in Florida and the Lizzie Borden House in Massachusetts. I believe we're all intuitive to some degree, but some have the gift more than others. For example, any one of us could play the piano—I could show you the three keys you need to press at the same time to make a

C-chord. But that doesn't make me Mozart. When it comes to psychics, it's the same thing—some folks truly have an intuitive gift. But I still listen to my gut. If I trust them, then I'm okay with using them in an investigation. To me, psychics are another tool in our arsenal to help verify what we're experiencing.

We never know for sure what's waiting for us when we reach out. I tell this to everyone, because it's so important. I don't care if you're using a Ouija board, a trigger object, or some fancy piece of technology. We know the history before we go into a location, to give us some kind of edge to know what we're dealing with, and we have all this equipment and these techniques for making contact. But still, that's only a start.

You just never know—could it be these things are now following us around? We know from experience that some entities know our names—we get them on our audio recorders and other devices. Could the entities at these locations have been told we were coming?

It's all possible. That's why it's important to be focused and have a strong mind before you go in. It's also critical to leave it behind when you leave. When you open a dialogue with whatever is on the other side, you might not like everything you hear . . .

. . . and sometimes, if your gut tells you to, you run! Fight or flight is a powerful human response to danger. I know we've been teased about making a run for it, but I won't apologize. When my body tells me to run, I'm going to run.

Always keep your guard up. Always.

CHAPTER 11

POSSESSION IN SAVANNAH

When I arrived in Savannah, Georgia, to investigate Moon River Brewery, I already thought this was one of the coolest cities in the world. The place is so rich in history: pirates, the Civil War, old shipyards, creepy old cemeteries. *Midnight in the Garden of Good and Evil* got it right. Cities have a vibe—you can feel it as soon as you walk down the street. You could be in a place for just two minutes and not even speak to anyone yet and just know—there's something to this place.

There was a time in my life when I had the opportunity to move to Savannah, but it fell through. Some cities keep calling you back. Maybe this trip back to film the Moon River Brewery was my destiny in some way.

I don't really believe in past lives, but Savannah has always seemed familiar to me. It's comfortable, but there is also an element of something dark hanging in the air. It's almost like being comfortable around your family while at the same time knowing their secrets.

My first impression of the building was, *Oh, boy. A restaurant. How haunted could this place be?* Maybe that's why I was so caught off guard during the lockdown.

ABOUT MOON RIVER BREWERY

The Moon River Brewing Company is in one of Savannah's oldest and most haunted buildings. Originally the site of the city's first hotel, the structure has survived hurricanes, the Civil War, and many angry ghosts who still roam free, attacking the staff and scaring those brave enough to enter after dark.

Built in 1821 by Charleston, South Carolina, native Elazer Early, the City Hotel was also home to the town's first branch of the United States Post Office and housed a branch of the Bank of the United States.

Though the City Hotel served the finest and most expensive wines, whiskeys, and brandies around to an affluent clientele, there was little to stop a patron from defending his honor to the death if he felt slighted. Southern honor was sacred, and duels were not uncommon. In the spring of 1832, a local undesirable named James Jones Stark was drunk and publicly insulted physician Dr. Philip Minis, calling him a "damn Jew" among other things.

Once again, on August 10, Stark began questioning Dr. Minis's honor at the bar in City Hotel. Dr. Minis walked into the bar, saw Stark, and claimed he saw the drunkard reach for his gun. So Dr. Minis drew his pistol and shot James Stark dead at the bar.

When Dr. Minis went to trial for the killing, it took the jury little time to acquit him of the crime. It seems locals were happy to see Stark gone, and they respected the doctor enough to keep him out of jail.

(Continued)

Another tale of mayhem involved a Mr. James Sinclair of New York City, who, according to a November 1860 *New York Times* article, headed south to Savannah aboard a steamship. He was out of work and hoped to find employment in Georgia. He was staying in the City Hotel when locals decided they didn't want some Yankee in their town. Sinclair was told to leave, but when he refused, he was dragged out of the hotel by a lynch mob, stripped, and beaten near to death.

Though locals weren't always friendly to City Hotel customers, the business remained in operation. The bar was full of fights and violence. The hotel finally closed in 1864 when General Tecumseh Sherman and the Union army marched through Georgia during the Civil War. There are rumors that the hotel became a makeshift field hospital for the retreating Confederate army, but by the time Sherman had reached Savannah, the town was mostly deserted and most of the buildings had been spared the Union's wrath. During Reconstruction, the former hotel sat unused and empty.

By 1900, the building was used as a lumber and coal warehouse; as the region's demand for coal diminished, the large building was used for more general storage. During the 1960s and '70s, 21 West Bay Street was an office supply store, until Hurricane David blew the roof off the building in 1979. In 1995 renovations began on the abandoned building and it saw new life as a brew pub when the Moon River Brewing Company opened its doors four years later.

Since its opening, the staff and customers of the restaurant and bar have encountered many unexplained and sometimes violent occurrences, including bottles being thrown at them by unseen forces. People have been touched, pushed, and slapped by the dark spirits who dwell inside. One of the most prominent ghostly figures is that of "Toby," a shadowy figure seen around the billiard room. This dark entity has been known to push patrons and staff.

The third floor isn't open to the public. It remains unfinished and untouched because, according to staff, construction workers are too scared to venture up there to renovate. A glowing white apparition has reportedly been seen on the upper floors and is believed to be that of a hotel worker who perished there many years ago.

During one attempt at renovation in the mid-1990s, a worker made up stories about the ghostly figure to scare the other workers, telling them she was a voodoo priestess. While he'd just fabricated the story, the spirit on the upper floors didn't take kindly to the tales. When the worker's wife came to visit the job site one afternoon, she was attacked and pushed down the staircase. The worker reportedly put in his resignation on the spot and fled the building. To this day, the upper floors remain in decay.

My first impression changed quickly when we took a daytime tour of the brewery's upper floors. I saw the decrepit hallways, the paint peeling off the walls, the dusty floors, and I thought, *Okay, this place has got a dark side too.*

The more we talked to employees, the more it became obvious that something bad was in the basement. Folks were afraid to go down there. Some of the female waitstaff had had their hair pulled by an unseen force, and other workers had seen dark shadow figures that scared the hell out of them. This place was getting more interesting by the second.

Walking around that building, I could sense the Civil War history, the battles, the turmoil. That stuff is soaked into the walls at the Moon River Brewery. But the basement . . . it was just weird down there. But I love being scared. I know it sounds odd, but I was getting psyched for the night's lockdown.

The restaurant closed early the night of our lockdown, which meant we would have the entire building to ourselves. Right after the manager locked us into the building, we headed in to set up our central base camp.

We were getting situated, unloading our gear, and I was filming the setup. Aaron and Zak were talking about the equipment when suddenly we heard what sounded like something heavy being dragged across the floor. It was loud and distinct, like a big chair or maybe even a person. Some old buildings creak and rattle on their own, but this wasn't like that. I've been in enough old structures to know the difference. This sound was unexplainable—and we hadn't been in the building more than a few minutes. I was kneeling down getting a shot of Aaron and Zak, and I almost fell over backward when I heard the sound.

We jumped up and I was pointing, *Go, go, go!* We all headed for the noise to check it out.

This was already an intense investigation. When the building acts up as soon as we walk in, it's going to be an interesting night. Little did I know just how interesting it would be for me personally.

As we got up to the second floor, where the sound was coming from, we couldn't find any cause for it. That's when we heard the same dragging sound coming from the third floor.

This was wild. My mind was running through all kinds of possibilities. Did someone from the restaurant stay behind and sneak upstairs to try to mess with us?

We raced up to the third floor now, looking for the cause of the dragging sound. When we got up there, the sound was gone and there was no sign of anyone. There's no way someone (living) could have snuck by us undetected. We hadn't been locked in more than ten minutes yet and already the building was acting up.

A short while later, when we officially started the investigation, we rolled our digital recorders and caught a sinister laugh right where we'd been standing before. Stuff like this freaks me out. It's validation that what I heard and the feelings I was having were real.

It seemed like the more we reached out to this entity, the more it reached back out to us. The feeling around us was intense. There was a kind of resonance to the building. It felt like there was the slightest vibration all around you, in the same way that if you've ever visited a battlefield or a murder scene, you can feel that something bad happened there.

That feeling got heavier and heavier around me. It was so slight that at first I didn't notice. I knew the presence was there, but it came on so slowly that I didn't feel it inside me yet. Only now with the benefit of hindsight can I see I was falling under the influence of this thing—whatever it was—in the Moon River Brewery.

We made our way down to the basement, where employees had been most afraid. I was already feeling drained, as if I'd been up for twenty-four hours. I shouldn't have felt this way—I was well rested and it wasn't that late yet, but I felt weak. Something was draining the life out of me.

In the basement I saw something white—like an old-time wedding dress, glowing—run by a doorway. I was feeling so tired, I accepted that maybe my eyes were playing tricks on me. But when you added everything up that had happened in the building already, you saw something really strange was occurring.

I can look back at the raw footage now and relive all of those moments. I can watch myself slowly come under the influence of whatever was there in the brewery.

By the time we got near the pool table in the basement, I was really distracted. We had already talked to people who had seen dark shadows down here, and the words of those employees were running through my mind. I thought about the devout Catholic woman who was down here screaming because of her experiences. The more uncomfortable I got, the more I felt myself slipping away.

I heard a scratching noise coming from right behind us. We all jumped. Next we heard the sounds of someone running toward us at full speed, getting closer and louder. It felt like we were about to get jumped by something. Suddenly I didn't care if it was a spirit or some living person who'd snuck into the building. We were about to get attacked. Zak and I were freaking out. But I was also just confused by the sound and entities surrounding me. I was dizzy, I was scared—and that was when my memory slipped away. From this point forward, I know only what you saw in the episode. It's me, but it's not me.

The best way I can describe this is that it's like one of those nights when you're totally exhausted and you go to bed. You lie down and fall asleep as your head hits the pillow. Suddenly your alarm goes off and it's morning. To you it feels like only a second has passed, though the clock shows it was eight hours. That's what I went through. My head was foggy; then it was over. When I came back to myself, all I could think was, *Shit! What just happened?*

When I watched the footage, I could see I was breathing heavily and my eyes looked different. It just wasn't me. I looked seriously pissed off. There was some other energy controlling me, but I was fighting against it inside—and I eventually won that fight, because the spell ended.

The entire event lasted maybe forty-five seconds. I came out of it confused, like I'd just woken up out of a deep sleep. I was groggy and bewildered. Forty-five seconds: not much time at all when you consider how much this changed the game for me.

The strangest part of watching the experience on-screen was seeing what looked like a shadow figure move out from behind me and then away. At the same time we captured an unexplained voice on the audio recorder. Right after Zak says, "They're right behind you," it sounds like a deep, hushed voice says, "I know." These three things—my blackout, the shadow figure, the disembodied voice—happening at once is more than coincidence.

What happened in the basement of the Moon River Brewery scared the shit out of me. The more it sank in, the more the whole thing unnerved me.

Many people have called this a possession, but that's not really how I look at it. I've done some research since then, and I believe this was more of an attachment.

People who study demons will tell you there are various types of ways entities can interact with living people, from mild influence to a full-on demonic possession (think of *The Exorcist* as the most extreme example). Some of these ways are:

Influence: An entity can influence our lives. It can offer temptations, and can even try to put thoughts into our heads.

Oppression: Oppression means that an entity has targeted a specific person and is not only trying to influence through temptation, but is also putting thoughts into our heads and trying to motivate our actions.

Attachment: The entity is now staying with us and tempting, oppressing, and even tormenting us. It can cause physical illness—something doctors can't cure—and it can cause depression.

Possession: Possession happens when the living person turns over control to the entity. This part is important—we all have free will. The only way a demon takes control is by invitation. Maybe the demon has promised money or fame or some other thing. This is the most rare phenomenon.

Looking back on Moon River Brewery, I feel that I went through a temporary attachment. I was an unwilling channel for the entity. That attachment didn't last for just the forty-five seconds or so that you saw; it went on for more than a week after.

This is the part of the experience we couldn't show on the episode.

Right after I came out of it in the basement, Zak and Aaron dragged me upstairs to where we had all our equipment. They were both freaking out. Aaron said, "What the fuck just happened?"

"Jesus, man, are you all right?" Zak asked.

To me, this was the most frightening part of the experience. All I was thinking was, *Kill you, kill you, kill you guys.* Zak didn't look like Zak to me; he was this weird figure. As drained as I was, I was also enraged. I looked at Aaron and I could think only about killing him. I told them both what was going through my head and they backed away from me and left me alone by the equipment for a minute. I'm sure they weren't far from me, and I'm positive they didn't have their backs to me.

Then Zak and Aaron heard something and moved toward the bar area.

That's when I snapped. I knew those thoughts I was having weren't my own. I knew I had been taken over by some entity in that building, so I grabbed my camera and started rolling as I made my way to the bar. "Fuck you!" I yelled. "You're going to do this shit to me?! I'm coming to get you now."

It's irrational, I know. I couldn't see this thing, but I knew it was around me somewhere. I wanted to fight, but on terms I could understand. I wanted to hit this thing and hurt it. I headed back downstairs to near the pool table. I went down alone. I didn't care—I wanted a piece of this thing.

I had never felt so violated in my life. I wanted revenge. Pure rage consumed my mind. From the stairway I heard both Zak and Aaron yelling at me: "Nick, get back up here!" A second later I heard them running down the stairs—they both knew I shouldn't be down there, especially alone.

They grabbed me and dragged me back upstairs to where I was able to get ahold of myself. The sun was going to rise soon; we had only about forty minutes before they were going to let us out. So from around two a.m., when I was overtaken, until about four a.m., all this crazy stuff was happening, but none of it made it into the episode.

Zak, Aaron, and I have had a lot of discussions about what

we do as investigators. I'm not a big believer in cleansing yourself or anything like that. In my experience, you need to leave these things where you find them. But I also got to thinking after Moon River that we go looking for these evil and dark entities at locations all over the place. When you do that, when you dance with the devil over and over again, eventually these things are going to take an active interest in you. This negative energy was starting to surround me. What happened in that basement was just the pinnacle of what I'd been doing for over a year at that point.

If we put out positive energy from ourselves, it forms a bubble that keeps the bad stuff out. I'm human, I don't feel positive all the time, so sometimes that positive energy I try to put out gets weaker and the bad stuff seeps in like a virus.

Now I know to work hard at putting out that positive energy, especially right after we finish a lockdown somewhere. Those are the days I need it most, so I can leave the bad stuff behind. Moon River Brewery taught me this tough lesson.

Up to that point, I thought this stuff couldn't happen to me. I wasn't even sure I believed it was possible at all. When I saw other people get overtaken, I thought they were either just faking it or under some kind of delusion. But this happened to *me*. If these entities can jump into my body, what else can they do? This shook me up, and it didn't end when we left the building.

Being locked in a morgue or sitting alone in a solitary confinement cell is just a scary dare. Having an unseen force take control of me was fucking frightening.

When I got home from Savannah, I felt nauseated for days. I was still shaken up and processing what I had gone through. Veronique noticed I was distant. I tried my best to explain what

I had gone through, but that would take time. I was still too close to the event.

Each day I worked to get my focus back—to try to increase that positive energy bubble around me. It seemed like each day was half as bad as the day before. After a little over a week, I could say that the attachment was over.

This wouldn't be my last brush with an entity trying to take control of me, but it taught me valuable lessons about staying focused during these investigations.

After Moon River Brewery, I have an understanding of how we can fall under the influence of entities that are out there around us. I was lucky because I had a strong will, mind, and spirit. Under different circumstances I may have needed some serious help fighting this thing.

Though I've had the chance to be in hundreds of these situations now, I still learn something new about the paranormal and about myself while doing this work. Every investigation changes me in some way, but a few leave a lasting impression—almost like a scar to remind me of what might be lurking around the next corner.

CHAPTER 12

FAVORITE CASES

Once we got past the first season of *Ghost Adventures*, investigating so many locations and living a life on the road was turning into something I loved. Getting off an airplane in a new place, seeing different landscapes, all of that is an adventure. Traveling allows you to connect with people because you voluntarily put yourself at their mercy. When you're in a strange town, you sometimes have no choice but to trust a stranger on advice like where to eat, where to shop, what local haunts to check out, and directions to the coolest bar in town.

Now that we all knew what we were doing, I could look forward to the locations and the lockdowns instead of worrying about every aspect of the production. The Travel Channel was pleased with the response from the first season, so this time they signed us up for seventeen episodes! That huge order was validation that this was way more than a good concept. That little idea Zak and I had kicked around was now beginning to look like a hit TV show.

Every location means something to me. We look at dozens of

potential sites before choosing one we feel is *Ghost Adventures* worthy. We look especially for places where dark, tragic events have taken place and where the spirit activity is malevolent. If people are being pushed, scratched, hit, or possessed by entities, we want to know about it.

Once we decide on a location, we really dig into it. Our researcher, Jeff Belanger, provides us with notes on the history, on what eyewitnesses have experienced, and where the hot spots are located. These notes get us ready for when we hit the ground.

Once you walk into a haunted location, you become part of that story forever. Given we're going in there to not only investigate, but film a television show, I recognize that I'm becoming a big part of the story of a haunted place. I take that seriously.

I know there are other ghost investigating shows out there—and I enjoy watching them! Really. Even though *Ghost Adventures* fans sometimes say, "Ooooooo," at the mention of another show, I have no beef at all. They do things their way; we do things our way. Watch both if you want different perspectives. There are some locations the other shows investigated first, and there are plenty where we investigated first. Our aim is the same. I am especially curious to see what the other guys find when they go to a place we've already been.

When you go looking for ghosts, sometimes you find something amazing and sometimes you get nothing. It's not fair to claim a place is haunted or not haunted based on a single visit. Some locations could be quiet for weeks, then be active for days at a time. We just don't know what's going to happen and when.

QUESTIONS FANS ASK

When you're in an old abandoned building, why do you think knocks and other strange sounds are ghosts and not rodents or birds?

I *do* assume that most bangs and knocks in old buildings have a natural cause. What you don't see on the show is how many times we debunk an odd noise. We'll hear some scratching sound coming from the wall, for instance. We're initially freaked out— it's dark, we can hardly see a thing, it's tense, and then there's this sound behind you. We turn on the flashlights and then see some big ol' raccoon in the next room scratching away. That stuff usually doesn't make it to the screen. What you see are the sounds we couldn't immediately find an explanation for. That doesn't mean it's paranormal; it just means we don't have an explanation for it.

Some of my favorite investigations involve locations that are big and decrepit. When I walk into these places, it's like stepping into a horror movie. Those old buildings come alive when I'm inside walking around in the dark. I tune in to them, they tune in to me. Here are a few of the locations that have been most important to me.

PENNHURST STATE SCHOOL

During the second season we had the chance to investigate the former Pennhurst State School in Spring City, Pennsylvania, just outside of Philadelphia. Rather than an actual school, Pennhurst was an institution for the mentally and physically disabled. I had seen pictures of this place and had heard about how some of the patients were tortured inside. The institution was controversial. It's been called "a monument to shame" because thousands of patients were abused over the almost eight decades the huge facility was in operation. At a quick glance, it almost looks like an old college campus. There are dozens of stately brick buildings, but today the trees and weeds are literally reaching up to engulf these structures as if nature were attempting to swallow this abomination.

The Pennhurst State School episode is one I'm most proud of because we were able to not only capture amazing evidence, but remind viewers of what can happen to people who sometimes don't have a voice. We even submitted this episode for an Emmy, but we didn't get a nomination.

ABOUT PENNHURST STATE SCHOOL

Even when Pennhurst was in full operation, these walls held something sinister. Ten thousand patients came through these doors, but not everyone left. Some were unwanted, others were thought to be beyond help, many suffered in conditions that were inhuman.

The horrid conditions the mentally and physically disabled patients were subjected to at Pennhurst pushed some of the staff and patients to the breaking point. Mistreatment, abuse, rape, and murder all took place in this vast network of buildings.

(Continued)

There's a scar that's been left here, and by many accounts it will never go away. It still lurks in these buildings.

In 1908, the state of Pennsylvania took a bold step in treating people with mental and physical disabilities by constructing a massive complex of buildings to house those with special needs. First called the Eastern Pennsylvania State Institution for the Feeble-Minded and Epileptic, the facility was quickly filled with adults and children of varying needs.

The patients were separated into different buildings based on their level of intelligence. Some people could mostly take care of themselves, but others were so profoundly disabled that they spent their days and nights in metal cribs, unable to wash themselves, and some could hardly turn themselves over.

Many heart-wrenching cases were brought to Pennhurst. Mentally retarded and autistic children were often dropped here at a young age because their families didn't know how to care for them. In many cases, the children never saw their families again—they were abandoned to become wards of the state.

Because of a lack of funding, the limited number of doctors, nurses, and orderlies could only do so much to help the suffering populace. Reportedly, some of the worst cases were starved so badly for any kind of human contact that they would smear themselves with their own feces so staff were forced to take care of them. The lack of staff also led to drastic measures in dealing with unruly patients. In some cases, people were drugged into submission or chained to their beds because the staff didn't have the resources or time to offer proper care.

Family members would visit their loved ones and find bruises, cuts, or much worse. Some patients were isolated for such long periods that they regressed; some even ceased talking. Some patients were killed by other patients—sometimes it was an accident; other times it was murder.

There were rules at Pennhurst. If a patient bit someone, they were punished. If they bit again, they were sent directly to the dentist's chair and had all of their teeth pulled. Scores of patients at Pennhurst had no teeth as a result of this extreme treatment. Thousands of teeth were pulled in a rusty dentist chair that still sits in the tunnels beneath the complex.

Exposés on the poor quality of treatment were written as early as 1912—just four years after the complex opened. But the abuse would continue for decades. In 1968, Philadelphia television news reporter Bill Baldini produced a multisegment exposé on Pennhurst called "Suffer the Little Children." The piece, with its powerful imagery of the suffering inside, drew the public's attention at last. Baldini did a real service with that piece, and I was proud to have him back for the episode of Ghost Adventures.

A massive lawsuit followed, further exposing some of the atrocities that had taken place at Pennhurst. In 1977, U.S. District Judge Raymond J. Broderick found the Pennhurst State School guilty of violating patients' constitutional rights.

The facility closed for good in 1987 and was left to decay. Up until a few years ago, it was owned by the Commonwealth of Pennsylvania and mostly neglected . . . and left to the ghosts, the angry spirits, the tormented victims who continued to inhabit the buildings and the land.

Once I knew about Pennhurst's past, I felt a lump in my throat. When I stood where these awful things had taken place, I thought I would cry. That powerful emotion would only get stronger as we interviewed people who used to work there, folks who could describe what Pennhurst was like in its day. Imagine putting a hundred profoundly retarded people into a room and just leaving them all day? They had no one to care for them, no interaction, and almost no supervision. Some were naked, some were violent, and many shut down. They weren't treated like humans, so they stopped acting like them.

It's easy to get angry at those who worked at Pennhurst, but that isn't the answer. Many of those employees—like the ones you saw us interview in the episode—were really good people who tried their best to help others, even to the point of volunteering on their days off. But one person can only do so much.

QUESTIONS FANS ASK

What's the most difficult part of paranormal investigations?

Communication with the other side and not knowing who you are speaking with. To me that is scary, because there are evil beings out there that can harm the living world. You need to keep a clear head and stay focused and balanced when talking to the spirit world so you can tell what's real from what may only be in your head.

By the time we interviewed former patient Betty Potts, I thought I was going to seriously break down. She's a wheelchair-bound woman who had been forced to come to Pennhurst when she was eight years old. When she described her life there, I felt tears welling up in my eyes as I tried to focus. She explained how they tied her down to her bed and placed her in seclusion. She would bang her head against the wall, she said, so she could get some attention from the staff. This poor woman—this human being like you and me—not only witnessed this, she lived through it.

When we were done interviewing her, I went outside to catch my breath and have some time alone for a minute. I glanced around at the buildings. These structures had been designed to help people, but instead became houses of torture. When you walk into a prison, you know what to expect—those people are there to be punished. But people went to Pennhurst because they needed help, at a school and hospital, a place for kindness and assistance. Instead they got torture.

Standing there at Pennhurst, glancing around, I realized that I—me, Nick Groff—am partially to blame for the type of abuse that went on there. And so are you. Because Pennhurst is an example of when society fails. When the institution was finally shut down, fingers were pointed in many directions, but the fault for the poor treatment lies squarely on the shoulders of society. Society didn't understand these disabilities, society didn't want to deal with these unfortunate people, and society didn't demand that their government allocate more resources for facilities like Pennhurst to take proper care of the people who needed the most help.

After those interviews and before the lockdown, Pennhurst became personal for me.

My mission was to tell the story here—not just the ghost story, but the personal story that represents the reason behind the haunting. That had always been the idea with *Ghost*

Adventures, but at Pennhurst this idea hit my heart. In that episode I felt I understood why this place was haunted. It *should* be haunted. Every soul who walks in there should be reminded of the screams from the past, and I wanted to remind our viewers of this too.

The Pennhurst campus was so huge that we rented a helicopter so we could film the place from above. It was eerie how vacant and hollow the place looked from above. As the helicopter came in for a landing, I felt myself reconnecting, getting mentally ready for this lockdown.

This location was a little different from the others. Because parts of the buildings are dangerous and falling apart, and because people are constantly trying to break into the buildings to thrill seek, vandalize, or steal scrap metal, we had security guards positioned outside for the entire night. In fact, the night before we arrived at Pennhurst, some kids had broken into one of the buildings and had to be chased out. And one time, one of those trespassers pointed a gun at the security guard. I swear, it's always the living you need to fear more than the dead. So we had a radio in case we needed help. The security guards locked us into the building for the night, so the only way to get around was through the underground tunnels that connect many of the buildings.

The tunnels beneath the buildings are so dark. Even if it's noon and sunny outside, these tunnels are black. As we were making our way down the passageway to the first building, I moved along the wall with only my night vision camera to light the way. I completely missed a metal chair lying on its side in front of me and I went tumbling over. A searing pain shot through my hand. After Zak shined his flashlight on me, I saw that my hand had just gone into broken glass and shards of metal on the floor. I saw the blood dripping down my arm. It hurt, and the worst part was I couldn't even remember the last tetanus shot I'd had. I made a mental note that I'd need to get one when I got back home. But I had to go on. We wouldn't get another shot at investigating this place.

The whole building had a feeling of sadness, but beyond the sadness, there was something else there. This sinister force. Something we didn't show on the episode was what happened to us on the top floor of the Mayflower building.

QUESTIONS FANS ASK

What are your top three most frightening moments on Ghost Adventures?

At the Washoe Club in Virginia City I heard my full name, "Nick Groff," come out in an EVP. That really freaked me out because the voice was so clear. At Moon River Brewery I was scared because I had never experienced something taking over my body like that before—I will never forget that. But my most frightening experience happened at Linda Vista Hospital when I locked eyes with a spirit. She still haunts me.

Some of the isolation rooms for the patients were on the top floor of the Mayflower. We were all hearing these voices. Now, part of the reason security was stationed outside all night was because they'd told us stories of finding trespassers in here before. So the only way in was through those tunnels—and right outside those locked tunnels were the security guards.

We'd heard enough disembodied voices on our investigations to know what was paranormal and what was not. The sounds we heard up there didn't seem paranormal at all. We heard voices, then the sounds of running feet. We were sure some kids were in there fucking with us. The more we listened, the more we were positive it was just some kids pulling a prank. Maybe they didn't even know we were there. I was pissed, you know? We were trying to investigate and film a show here. I started yelling, "Hey—we're calling security if you don't get in here right now!"

The voices and running continued, so we got on the walkie-talkie and asked security to come up and deal with this. On the episode you don't get to see what happens next. Security unbolted the door and ran a pretty good distance to come find us.

They did a sweep throughout the building and found nothing—not a trace of any break-in, not a soul. And there was no way out except through the tunnel we'd come in! Now we were a bit freaked out. These guys shrugged their shoulders and said, "It happens here." Then they walked out and locked us inside again.

We didn't collect a ton of evidence at Pennhurst, but there was this overwhelming feeling of sadness all around. The most interesting paranormal occurrence was when a rock was thrown at us by an unseen force. We caught the small stone bouncing by on camera. Though the paranormal activity on the night of our lockdown wasn't as intense as other locations, Pennhurst will haunt me forever. I'm fortunate to have had the chance to investigate there and proud of the story we could bring to light again. We can never have enough reminders that we must take care of our fellow human beings.

GHOST HUNTING IN ITALY

Poveglia Island was another location I had heard about years before. Located off the coast of Venice, this place seemed like it could be one of the creepiest locations on earth. We tried to go there during our first season, but foreign travel and filming can be very expensive, so our budget didn't allow for it. During season two, Zak and I pushed to get there. I'm glad we did.

ABOUT POVEGLIA ISLAND

Off the coast of Venice, Italy, there Is an island that legend says was formed from the ashes of all the dead who were buried there. Poveglia was once home to an Insane asylum, but today the entire island is abandoned.

Locals and tourists alike are forbidden from setting foot on the island. Fishermen avoid the area because they say it's cursed. Poveglia Island *is* Italy's darkest haunt.

In the south lagoon between Venice and Lido sits this small island that has been a place of refuge, a stronghold, and a dumping ground for the sick, dying, and deceased for many centuries.

In AD 421, Poveglia Island saw its first inhabitants arrive. Barbaric invaders had come to the mainland, so locals took their boats to the nearby island for protection. The island was highly defendable and, considering its relatively small size, not worth the trouble for invading armies.

(Continued)

In 864, two hundred followers of Doge Pietro Tradonico settled on the island after Tradonico was assassinated by Italian nobles. For centuries the small group managed the island and avoided many taxes and laws that would have applied to them on the mainland. The population dwindled and eventually the island was abandoned in the fourteenth century.

When the bubonic plague arrived in Venice in 1348, many islands, including Poveglia, became lazarettos—or quarantine colonies. Venice was particularly harsh in dealing with the infected. When citizens showed signs of the plague, they were carted off—against their will—to islands like Poveglia. This was almost certainly a death sentence.

Near the center of the island the dead, or those too sick to protest, were burned in giant pyres. The corpses of tens of thousands of those who'd perished in Venice made their way to the Poveglia pyres.

The bubonic plague killed one out of three Europeans. People lived in constant fear. Families turned on one another as the dying lay in torment. But 1348 wasn't the last plague to hit Venice. In 1630 another disease spread through the city. Again the nearby islands like Poveglia were used for the sick and dying. There was so much death that a psychic scar was left on the region forever. Ghostly reports on the island go back centuries.

Between 1798 and 1801, during Napoleon's military campaign through Italy, he used Poveglia Island as a place to store gunpowder and weapons. He knew that between the ghostly legends and the island's defendable position, his weapons cache would be safe.

In the late 1800s, an asylum was constructed on Poveglia Island. Isolated from Venice and from the world, the mentally disturbed couldn't bother anyone else. Likewise, there was very little oversight in regard to the facility's caregivers. Locals will tell you the rumors about a doctor in the 1930s who conducted strange experiments on patients, butchering his victims. The doctor eventually went mad, and jumped from the tall bell tower. Though the bell in the tower was removed decades ago, locals still report hearing a chime echoing from the old tower.

By the mid-twentieth century, the facility had been converted into a geriatric center for the elderly to live out their final days. The place closed for good in 1975, leaving only the shell of the building behind to remind us of what was once there.

In recent years, construction crews attempted to restore the former hospital buildings. But, inexplicably, the crews stopped working, leading some to speculate that they were driven away by some dark force on the island.

Poveglia is an island—it's surrounded by water. Like many investigators, I believe there is a connection between water and the paranormal. These spirits, these entities seem to be trapped here, unable to cross the watery plane. Maybe the water amplifies the activity here—it's a theory we'd be able to test during our lockdown.

None of us speaks Italian, so there was a language barrier here. But we learned a few phrases before the investigation. One key phrase: *Usa la mia energia*, or "use my energy." While trying to record spirit voices there, I was curious if we'd capture EVP sounds and if the words would be in English or Italian.

QUESTIONS FANS ASK

Why don't you guys use your thermal camera more often than your other gear?

We use the thermal camera quite a bit—almost in every location. The reason you don't see it in every show is because sometimes we don't capture anything. Sometimes we'll let that thing roll for an hour, looking in every corner of a building, and get nothing. We're not going to bore the viewers with that. But then again, sometimes we capture some amazing footage with the thermal.

In the Gettysburg episode we captured that dark blue human-looking figure down near the train tracks. The blue color means the figure was colder than the environment around it. At the Amargosa Opera House and Hotel we saw that reddish-colored figure move out of one of the rooms. We believe that red color meant the spirit was sinister.

At the Hales Bar Marina we captured a solid-looking figure up near one of the locks standing by Aaron. So the thermal can be an amazing piece of investigation equipment, but we don't get results with it at every location.

This lockdown was also different for us in that there were no doors to lock us in with. Well, we'd been dropped off by boat for the night, so if we wanted to leave, we'd be making a swim for it. Now that's a true lockdown.

Usa la mia energia became a point of contention between me and

Zak at Poveglia. Zak would yell back at me, "No! Don't say that." He didn't think it was a good idea to allow these spirits to use our energy. I should mention here that we had machetes to get around the island because the vegetation was so thick in some places.

One weird thing was that there was no electricity running to this island, yet we were getting EMF readings, and the batteries on my camera were being sucked dry. When that happens, I feel like something big is on the horizon. Soon it wasn't just my batteries—I felt the energy draining out of me. I was getting dizzy and nauseated, and then I saw that it wasn't just me. Aaron and Zak were also feeling strange. It hit us all at the same time. Then Zak started to get into this prepossessed stage. Something was attaching itself to him. Shit was getting weird now and we had nowhere to run.

Zak started going nuts and was hitting the wall. I'd been through this before. I could see we needed to get Zak out of this room right away before there was a full-on attachment. He was going into a blind rage . . . and the dude had a machete strapped to his side. I pulled him out of the room so he could get some air.

I was getting really uncomfortable at this point. There were only three of us on the entire island, we were all feeling drained, and now Zak was about to have an attachment. There was no exit plan.

Once Zak was outside and settling down, I felt a little better. But, crap, we were in a foreign country and didn't speak a word of the language. On that tiny haunted island I'd never felt so far from home and safety.

Once we'd split up to take solo vigils, the location got even more intense for me. When I went into the ruins of the main hospital building, I stood still for only a few moments to let my eyes adjust. Some ambient light came in through the windows— just enough so I could see shadowy figures moving around in the dark. There's no fear compared to when you know you should be alone but you realize you're not.

Our best capture of this investigation happened when I was in that hospital building. Sure enough, our night vision camera caught a shadowy figure darting by, which validated what I was seeing. I'm always blown away when the evidence backs up our own personal experiences.

I've never felt so grateful to see the sun breaking on the horizon as I was the next morning on Poveglia Island. In some respects, this location was easier for me to put behind me. Something about the island made these entities feel isolated to me, as if I knew they couldn't follow me. They were stuck there, thousands of miles away in the Laguna Veneta.

QUESTIONS FANS ASK

Is there a location you'd really like to do a lockdown?

Since our first season I've wanted to investigate the Kings Park Psychiatric Hospital on Long Island, New York. This giant hospital closed in 1996 after more than a century of operation. The big abandoned buildings just speak to me.

RETURN TO THE WASHOE CLUB

The Washoe Club in Virginia City keeps calling me back. As I've said, I feel some kind of personal connection with this place. The more I go there, the more I feel like I should go back.

The strangest experience I had inside this storied building didn't happen as part of a *Ghost Adventures* episode, though.

It happened during a paranormal event we held in town for our fans, in October 2007.

One of the highlights was taking the attendees into the Washoe Club with us for a séance. There were about twenty of us sitting in a circle in the upstairs ballroom, which was the exact spot where I'd caught that apparition for the documentary. EVP specialists Mark and Debby Constantino were there, as was Janice Oberding, a longtime author and paranormal researcher who's been on a couple of *Ghost Adventures* episodes. And my friend Dave Schrader from Darkness Radio was sitting next to me.

The group took up the whole ballroom. We were all holding hands and getting quiet. I'm not usually one for séances, but I figured if I was going to try this, then I was really going to focus. I concentrated on my spiritual side.

Pretty soon different women in the circle claim they're being touched. One woman says her hair was just pulled; another says she just got her hair yanked. These women aren't even sitting next to each other—they're spread around the circle. Whatever this thing is around us, it's getting more aggressive.

"So, you want to be a tough guy?" Dave Schrader calls out.

I jump in: "All you can do is push girls? What's up with that?"

Together, Dave and I say, "Why don't you do something to us?"

I look over to the hallway next to the ballroom—exactly where I'd been right before I'd caught that apparition—and I see a man standing there leaning against the doorway. I know this is in my mind's eye because no one else is reacting to it. He's looking at me—it's like he knows that I see him. He kind of looks like that creepy old guy in *Poltergeist II*—the black hat and clothes, but not as old. When I see this figure I feel like I'm going to throw up. My head starts sweating, and the room feels like it's going to spin on me. I keep seeing flashes of this guy—almost like a strobe effect.

Aaron is standing across the room from me—he doesn't participate in séances like this—and has a clipboard tucked under his arm. Suddenly the clipboard comes out from under his arm and goes flying down the hallway, like someone's just grabbed it and thrown it. I'm thinking, *Holy crap*.

I get up, Dave gets up, people are getting hurt, I'm getting sick, and I want this to be over. We are all unnerved, so we break the circle and the activity dies down.

This was that moment when I knew that the spirits knew me there. And I knew them.

I would be validated when Mark and Debby Constantino went there for their own investigation years later. They captured EVP that had my full name, "Nick Groff," even though I was hundreds of miles away at the time. So it was a no-brainer for us to go back and film another episode here in season three.

I know I'll be back there again and again. I don't know when, but it's destiny when it comes to the Washoe Club.

LIVE FROM THE TRANS-ALLEGHENY LUNATIC ASYLUM

Early on during the filming of season two, we knew we had a hit show. Our ratings were solid, and the Travel Channel was thrilled to be working with us. That's when the network brought up the idea of doing a live Halloween special. In the past, they had done this with the *Most Haunted* program from the UK, and this year it would be our turn.

The concept was a seven-hour live program where we

investigated a location. I didn't even have to think about it. I believe my exact answer was, "Oh, hell yeah!" I looked at this as a new challenge. The only part of live television that concerned me was the technical aspect: How would we cut from one camera to another? How would we transition? And what other elements could we bring in?

Doing what we do live wouldn't be any different for me because during our lockdowns we only ever get one take at capturing paranormal phenomena. The cameras are always rolling, and we're always ready for what might happen.

But—and it's a big but—I also know that hours can go by when nothing happens. I know from filming our lockdowns that setting up our equipment and base camp isn't riveting television. When we walk from one section of a building to another, it's just walking. No one wants to watch that. This live show would take some planning.

We kicked around a few different location ideas but eventually decided on the Trans-Allegheny Lunatic Asylum in Weston, West Virginia. The place is huge and haunted—and, come on, it's a former asylum. That's GAC all the way.

The building itself presented some technical issues. Because the walls were so thick, we wouldn't be able to use wireless cameras to send the signal to the broadcast booth. And the building is huge, which meant we would need miles of cables for everything.

That also meant that the three of us would need to have cables dragging behind us. I wasn't happy about that, because when you have thirty or forty feet of cable behind you it can get caught on things like doors and chairs and cause dragging noises far away from you. But there was no other way in this case. We would have to work around it.

On each floor, Aaron and I would have to plug into a wire in a predetermined position. Those transitions had to happen quickly. We decided we would preproduce short segments ahead of time to play during those transitions. The segments would include interviews with witnesses who had had experiences in the sections of the building we were about to investigate.

To help us out during the investigation, we brought in some of our friends and leading experts in the field. We had psychic Chris Fleming, Mark and Debby Constantino, *Ghost Adventures* fans who were going to join us for part of the lockdown, and a support staff inside to review our evidence as we gathered it.

ABOUT TRANS-ALLEGHENY LUNATIC ASYLUM

In 1858, workers broke ground on an ambitious new building complex: the Trans-Allegheny Lunatic Asylum. For the next twenty-three years, employees toiled to construct the largest hand-cut stone masonry building in North America. Earlier, in 1848, psychologist Dr. Thomas Kirkbride had developed an asylum design that revolutionized care for mentally challenged people. Instead of locking these folks in prisons or chaining them up in basements like some dirty family secret, Dr. Kirkbride proposed that sprawling campuses be built that could be self-sufficient. Staff, and some patients, would grow their own food, make clothes, and cook their own food. Kirkbride's plan worked. When the mentally challenged were treated like human beings, they enjoyed some happiness and learned some skills. The plan was copied all over the United States and soon there were more than a dozen Kirkbride hospitals in America.

Following the Kirkbride plans for mental asylums, the Weston facility featured expansive wings in a staggered formation, which allowed as much sunlight and moving air as possible for the patients inside. Originally designed for 250 people, the complex reached its peak population in the 1950s, when numbers swelled to 2,400 patients in overcrowded and poor conditions.

This impressive campus of buildings found itself caught in the crossfire during the U.S. Civil War. Construction had begun using Virginia funds, but when West Virginia seceded from the Confederacy to join the Union, construction was halted and the grounds were used for training soldiers to fight for the North. Today there's a Civil War wing of the building that appears to be active with spirits from that era.

Construction was completed after the Civil War and the building was renamed the West Virginia Hospital for the Insane.

As with so many Kirkbride hospitals, Trans-Allegheny went from cutting-edge and humane treatment, to overcrowded conditions, to underfunding, and finally to ruin. In 1994, the building closed its doors, leaving the paint to peel, the wood to rot, and the metal to rust. But even before the doors were locked, staff knew there were more patients present than they could account for. Nurses reported hearing disembodied footsteps and the cries of mentally tormented patients.

(Continued)

In recent years, the Trans-Allegheny Lunatic Asylum has enjoyed a rebirth as a tourist destination. Though the building offers historical tours during the daytime, it's the evening ghost hunts that bring in visitors from all over the world. With so many people in anguish while the place was open, it's no surprise that ghostly accounts still pour out of the giant compound. Many of the hauntings seem to be residual, a kind of psychic imprint left there. In fact, residual hauntings are the most common kind. It's not a trapped spirit, it's not interactive, it's just a sort of memory of the location.

There are accounts of these types of hauntings at Trans-Allegheny, but there are also stories of dangerous interactions with spirits. One tour guide was assaulted by an unseen force in the stretcher room of the main building. She was pinned down and flailing when two of her friends came to her rescue. There are still rooms and hallways that staff and tour guides avoid. Every part of this building has some reported activity, and though some seem to be benign former patients, others are out to harm.

Asylums are havens for negative energy. All of that torment and human drama leave a stain. The conditions inside Trans-Allegheny were sometimes inhumane. I spoke with one former volunteer who told me how, when she was counseling a patient going through an alcohol rehab program, she watched cockroaches crawling out from under his sleeves. The place was so dirty that patients didn't even bother to wipe the bugs away anymore.

QUESTIONS FANS ASK

If you could get an EVP from one person from history, who would it be and what would you ask them?

I was so close to my grandmother that I'd probably reach out to her spirit and ask her what happens after you pass on from this world. I'll admit I'm afraid to actually try this because I don't want her spirit to linger.

Doing the live show here was exhilarating for me. I loved the pressure of no second chances, of everything having to work properly the first time. During the episode viewers were asked to text in where they wanted to see me get locked in alone. The choice was between two buildings and the former morgue. Of course the viewers picked the morgue. More than five hundred thousand people texted in to vote.

That night we captured multiple EVPs on our digital recorders and were able to play them live during the show. We also had personal experiences like cold spots, and during one session with Chris Fleming, Zak heard an audible spirit voice next to his ear.

After seven live hours, all the amazing feedback, and the thrill of seeing it all come together, I was beginning to understand just how popular we were with fans.

People could connect with us because we're just regular guys who put themselves in extreme situations. When it's scary, we freak out. We're not afraid to laugh at ourselves, and we're willing to go the distance when it comes to exploring the most extreme haunts around.

FUN AND PRANKS ON LOCATION

It's not all demons and tense moments on *Ghost Adventures* shoots. We have a lot of fun too. If you check out Aaron's vlogs on our YouTube channel (www.youtube.com/gaccrew) or at my channel (www.youtube.com/NickGroffVlogs), you can see hundreds of our wackier moments.

When you're sitting around all day waiting for equipment to arrive, or interview subjects to show up, or you're stuck in a hotel, you need to amuse yourself.

BOOM AUDIO HELP

During our shoot at Letchworth Village in New York, Zak was sitting in the front seat of the rental car trying to record voice-overs for an episode we'd already shot. With Aaron rolling his camera, I walked up to the car carrying a boom mic and dropped it over the car near the windshield so it looked like I was trying to record Zak's audio through the glass. Aaron came around to the passenger window to catch Zak's reaction. The whole goal was to break his concentration. At first Zak started to smile as he was trying to read a serious voice-over. Then he started to laugh. Aaron and I were cracking up. When Zak came out for a mock-interview, I kept rubbing the big fuzzy mic against his face until he chased me off.

COOKIE TIME

For our Valentine's Day special at Longfellow's Wayside Inn in Sudbury, Massachusetts, we were staying at a nearby hotel that put out cookies in the lobby for the guests. It's not like they said, "Just take one," so I took the whole plate. It was almost one a.m. and Aaron filmed me walking down the hall with the plateful of cookies. I knocked on Zak's hotel room door and handed him a cookie. Then I started placing chocolate chip cookies at the doorways to other people's rooms. We were all trying not to burst out laughing. It was so late, and even though most of the rooms around us were taken by people in our production crew, we didn't want to wake anyone else up. We were tired from a long day of filming and everything was funny at that point. The more we tried not to laugh, the funnier everything was. Everyone who's seen this video on YouTube thinks we were all stoned. I promise you we weren't—we were just giggly for a late-night snack. Cookie, anyone?

SKELETON ZAK

When we filmed Execution Rocks Lighthouse near New York City, we had a skeleton for a prop. The night before we started filming, we'd all gone to a Korean barbecue joint and Zak got serious food poisoning; I got a mild case of it. Zak was puking his guts out for two days. So I put this skeleton's arm around my shoulder, then put Zak's sunglasses on the skeleton. In the vlog you can watch me talking to "Skeleton Zak" about all the weight he's lost in the last forty-eight hours. Zak moves the skeleton's mouth with his finger as we talk about how thin he looks.

(Continued)

ROOM SERVICE

When we were staying in Jerome, Arizona, to investigate the Jerome Grand Hotel and the former Club House Hospital, Aaron decided to intrude on us. First Aaron walked in with his camera rolling as I was getting changed. I thought it was pretty funny. Then both of us went to Zak's door, and I pretended to be room service. Zak answered the door half naked, then slammed the door in our faces. He was furious it was us. Aaron and I couldn't stop laughing. Man, being on the road so much can make you punch-drunk sometimes.

CHAPTER 13

LINDA VISTA HOSPITAL: THE GAME CHANGER

Once we were into the routine of filming season two of *Ghost Adventures*, I didn't think there were any surprises left for me to discover when it came to ghosts. We'd investigated eight locations in the first season and had already been to a dozen more in 2009, so by now this was my full-time occupation. In so many respects it was a dream come true—working full-time in TV production and exploring my favorite topic: the paranormal. I had no idea when I arrived in East Los Angeles, California, on July 29, 2009, that my life was about to change permanently. Dreams sometimes contain nightmares.

On that sunny July day I had already accepted the fact that ghosts exist. I had encountered them, I'd captured plenty of evidence supporting the fact that they are here, but I didn't understand exactly *what* they were. It made sense that a lot of this stuff was something residual—a scene that had played out in the location at one time and now plays over and over like movie. I could buy that. I also accepted the fact that maybe some things were a projection of the mind—sometimes my mind, and sometimes another living person's mind—even to the point where multiple people could witness the same thing. Having had the attachment experience back in Moon River Brewery, I also believed that there are masses of energy out there that can influence us. But the intelligent spirits—the ones that can communicate with you and respond to direct questions—I wanted to learn more about these entities. They are the most rare and the most elusive.

The encounter at Linda Vista Hospital was different from any other experience I'd had before. This contact made me rethink everything. It scared the hell out of me. I still shudder when I relive that moment—those two seconds that changed everything.

I first heard about Linda Vista from my cousin Justin. He's always a world of information. He'd told me about an abandoned hospital that was now being used for movies and television shows because it's in Los Angeles. I wondered how such a place could remain standing in an area where real estate must be at a premium, but once I saw it, I understood—not even an Oscar-winning Hollywood set designer could build a set this creepy and realistic. The place is gigantic, and you can visualize what it must have been like when the place was open and running as a hospital twenty-four/seven.

I've got a couple of friends I play basketball with in Las Vegas who grew up in East LA. They knew about Linda Vista Hospital, and told me how the whole area is controlled by gangs. They warned me it was a rough neighborhood. I wasn't too worried about it; nobody really bothers us when we're out filming. Especially if they realize there's a chance they'll be on television.

After being inside so many abandoned buildings I realized that buildings are entities unto themselves. The walls, floors, ceilings,

ABOUT LINDA VISTA HOSPITAL

Hospitals are built for the sick and suffering. For many, these places are the last stop on the way to the morgue. When you consider the rough East Los Angeles neighborhood surrounding the former Linda Vista Hospital, it's no surprise that this building has seen a heavy death toll, which may help to explain why it's considered to be such an active and dark haunt today.

First established in 1904 as the Santa Fe Coast Lines Hospital, the building was constructed to service Santa Fe Railroad employees. In the early decades of the twentieth century, Linda Vista grew and prospered as did the surrounding Boyle Heights neighborhood. It was rebuilt and greatly expanded in 1924, responding to the rising need for a bigger hospital in the area, and the facility prospered. A nurses' dormitory was added with a tunnel connecting it to the main hospital.

In 1937, the hospital changed its name to the Linda Vista Community Hospital. After the Great Depression and then World War II, East Los Angeles slowly transformed into a less affluent area. As the surrounding neighborhoods declined, the amount of violent crime rose. Linda Vista served everyone in its surrounding community, but in the 1970s and 1980s gangs moved into the region, bringing a significant increase of gunshot wound, stabbing, and beating victims into the ER. Hundreds died here in recent decades.

Some of the dead were gangbangers, some were innocent

(Continued)

victims of violent crimes, and others were the area's sick. Many were brought to Linda Vista who didn't survive.

With so many poor and uninsured patients, Linda Vista Hospital struggled to stay afloat. By 1988, the hospital was forced to stop accepting ambulances in its emergency room because the facility was understaffed and the majority of patients couldn't pay for services. A downward spiral had begun. Conditions inside deteriorated, the best doctors moved on to better hospitals, and the death toll continued to rise as the quality of care worsened.

Officially the hospital closed because of lack of funds, though some locals will tell you it was because the doctors were mistreating patients, causing an unusually high fatality rate.

In 1991, the last patient checked out of Linda Vista. The buildings began the rapid deterioration that comes with sitting empty. The hospital may have been lost forever if not for Hollywood. Several movies used parts of the building as a set. Scenes of blockbusters like *Outbreak*, *End of Days*, and *Pearl Harbor* were filmed inside Linda Vista, as was the pilot episode for *ER*.

During these productions, Linda Vista's ghostly reputation grew. Because of the expensive equipment left on the first floor during filming, security guards were hired to watch the grounds and sets overnight. They chased many a darting shadow and heard cries that unnerved some to the point of quitting their jobs.

Though there are hundreds of accounts of dark, shadowy

figures lurking the halls and rooms of the complex, there are a few spirits who seem to still be victims. A little girl's ghost—perhaps an innocent victim of a violent crime—has been spotted in the surgical area. A young woman's ghost has been seen on the third floor—maybe unaware that she has died. And an older orderly figure has been seen walking the halls, still tending to his duties though the patients and staff are long gone.

Those ghosts aren't hurting anyone. Yet there are other, darker entities sneaking through doorways and hiding in dark corners of the building. People have been touched, pushed, and frightened out of their wits.

decorations, and even furniture hold an imprint of human activity. When a building is in use—whether it's an office or store or house—there's a feeling to the place. It's somehow alive. When a building sits empty for years, it's a different feeling. Call it an irrational personification if you want, but I've felt it. The abandoned places seem to *want* humans inside.

I felt that yearning as soon as I walked into this hospital. I had no expectations that this would be any different from any other location we'd investigated, but once I got inside I felt a chill—like I knew this place was haunted.

I could imagine gang members from Compton and East LA being shuttled in through these doors, bleeding from stab wounds or gunshot wounds. Illegal immigrants turned away because they couldn't afford medical treatment, left to rot and die in waiting rooms and on the sidewalks. And perhaps worst of all, the rumors of inept medical staff offering the promise of hope and healing, only to cause even more pain, suffering, and death.

Linda Vista was our first investigation inside a medical hospital. It wasn't just dark, foreboding energy we'd be encountering there; there was the possibility of something positive being retained as well, since hospitals can sometimes be a place for joy as well.

During our walk-through of the building, we saw the incinerator where they used to cremate the bodies of John and Jane Does. Zak put his hand in the little box, still full of human ash and bone. That freaked me out. "What are you doing?" I said, with a mischievous grin on my face. Human remains were still here!

As I was filming the eyewitness interviews, I felt like something was watching us, kind of lurking in the wings and checking us out. It wasn't a feeling I'd experienced strongly before at other locations. Usually the paranormal events happened for me only during the lockdowns—when I was looking for it.

The stories the eyewitnesses shared would send a chill down anyone's back. Being pushed by unseen hands, hearing disembodied voices humming during EVP sessions—this place was clearly very active. And of course, when we went outside, the tour guide showed us what Zak called "the cherry on the sundae": Linda Vista also had a mental ward on its grounds. I can still see Zak's eyes get large in excitement when we found out about that.

While we were interviewing two women who had captured some intriguing examples of EVP there, we decided to conduct a real-time EVP session of our own. It was the first time we ever tried it during the daytime, when we weren't in lockdown mode. It was in the same trauma room where the women had captured their evidence, and indeed we captured the same sort of female humming noises that they'd caught. We'd been recording for only a minute or two, and there it was, sounding eerily similar to what they had caught before. We were so pumped—you could just tell there was something in that trauma room. In fact there were two trauma rooms side by side, and both of them were charged with spirit energy. With all the people who lived out their last moments in those rooms, and even those who made it out of there alive, so much of their energy must be imprinted inside.

The walk-through and all the eyewitness testimony got us even more excited for the lockdown. We strategized how best to go about the investigation—I mean, this place was huge, and it seemed like there were reports of paranormal activity in almost every nook and cranny of the facility. It certainly didn't disappoint us either—we got activity pretty much from the start. Even as we were setting up our static night vision cameras, we were getting anomalies appearing on the footage and EVPs coming through on the camera audio and on our digital recorders.

During the investigation, we started off in the main hospital before traveling to the mental ward via the underground tunnel that connected the two buildings. Even there, we were getting some good stuff. But when we came back into the main hospital, that's when the activity intensified. We started with the top floors and worked our way down to the first floor. I could feel the energy building as the night progressed. We went from capturing EVPs to hearing things with our own ears—creepy voices and weird, unexplainable sounds, like someone breathing through an oxygen mask.

We entered the trauma rooms, and at this point I had my digital audio recorder as well as my camera going. I was standing in the place where so many victims had been laid out to await treatment. Straight in front of me was the corridor where the nurses and doctors would come in to get their tools, wash their hands, and prep for tending to their patients. Zak was standing in that corridor, filming me. I stepped in front of the room where we had captured the voice during the walk-through, and Aaron came into the other room behind me as well. My eyes began to adjust to the dark; the LCD from the camcorder was illuminating the room a bit too. I started my digital recorder and was starting to go through my whole spiel of setting up the recording for the session; telling the spirits I'm there to communicate. I looked to my left and saw nothing in the darkness. All I could see was the trauma center. But as soon as I turned my head back the other way—*boom!* There was a woman standing literally two feet in front of my face.

Our eyes connected, and for once in my life I felt pure, unadulterated fear. This woman was a solid figure, but her face glowed slightly, which is why I could see her so clearly in the dark. Her skin was pale white, she had brown eyes and short brown hair, and she was wearing a hospital gown. The gown had a small floral pattern like you see on so many hospital gowns. I'll never forget that detail. I have no way of knowing for sure, but she had kind of a 1980s/early 1990s look to her. I saw her. She saw me. We locked eyes—a deep psychic connection happened. She shouldn't be standing there, but she was.

When I saw her, it felt as if time had frozen. But on the video, you see me jump back very quickly, no more than two seconds. To me, it felt like a minute or two where this girl and I were just staring at one another. She reached out her arm, trying to touch me just as I was turning away. I saw her lean forward with her head slightly tilted down, and her eyes gazed up at me. It was like she was sad and reaching out for help, angry that nobody could help her.

I don't care how tough you think you are—if you see something like that, it's going to freak you out. You'll be startled, you'll jump, no matter who you are.

The sensation was like free falling but never being able to hit the ground. My heart pounded like it was going to burst out of my chest. You know all those urban legends about when a person sees a ghost, and their hair turns all white and a terrified expression is permanently frozen on their face? I thought that was going to happen to me. Every nerve in my body was on fire—I had to get away from this spot now!

The reaction I had, which Zak captured on his camera, shows the raw emotion that I felt. I can laugh at it now, but at the time, that was the face of true terror. People have criticized our show and the whole reality television genre for being forced and contrived, but there's nothing more real than the reaction I had. That is pure reality TV right there. I couldn't fake that for you now if I tried.

I don't remember much of my retreat from this woman. I saw on the footage that I pushed past Aaron to get away from her as quickly as I could. I made it to the hallway, where I started having a total freak-out. Once I'd settled down a bit, we reviewed the footage to see if we'd caught anything. What we saw on tape was nearly as mind-blowing as actually seeing her with my own two eyes.

I had a camera facing in the direction of where the woman materialized, as did Aaron. Zak's was facing me, filming me. So, both my and Aaron's cameras were pointed in her direction, and right at the moment of the manifestation, they both froze.

It's like whatever energy was there knocked out the magnetic part of our mini-DV tapes and froze the film reels in time, and then picked up again once she was gone. My camera stopped right when I saw her; Aaron's froze a split second later. It was like an energy burst had hit my camera first, then struck his, and then went out into the hallway. I still can't understand how it happened, but I'm convinced it was so that we wouldn't capture what I saw on film. It was meant for only me to see.

With all the ghost hunting groups out there looking for this stuff with cameras rolling, why are the experiences so rarely captured on tape? You might get orbs, light anomalies, EVPs, or whatever, but full-bodied apparitions are so rarely captured.

I don't think we've gotten far enough with the science or technology yet. The equipment can't yet validate what we are experiencing with our human senses. We use only such a small percentage of our brains. Many feel that there is an extra "sixth sense" that allows us to perceive ghosts. How can we expect technology to pick up on that, when it can't even correctly convey the five senses that we've already proven exist?

Once I'd gathered myself together, we decided that we had to go back to the surgery area. I wasn't okay yet. It would take weeks to process what had just happened to me. But as frightened as I was, I wanted to know more about this woman.

When something scares you that much, a lot of people ask, how do you go back into the location and continue the investigation? The only answer I can give is that you just do it. You mentally push yourself, will yourself to do it. It took me a little while, but once I'd calmed down I reminded myself that this was why I was here.

I couldn't go back into the room where I saw the girl, but I got as close as the room that Aaron had been standing in. Zak slid an audio recorder, then a PX device into the trauma room. He was holding the PX in phonetic mode and asked, "Did we just see you?" and the PX responded immediately with, "Yeah, you did." When he asked the follow-up question, "What do you want us to do?" the PX responded with, "Leave." The last word the PX said was, "Dead." After we let a static night vision camera roll for an hour in the surgical suite where I'd seen the woman, we captured one faint voice that eerily cried out something like, "Don't leave me."

What didn't make it into the episode happened about an hour after my encounter with the woman. I stayed in the hallway outside the surgical suite by myself while Zak went to the morgue and Aaron went to the boiler room. At first, I was standing in the room where Aaron was filming when my encounter happened, but then I started inching my way toward the surgery room where I had seen the girl. I didn't want to go in; I just wanted to be able to see in there. I could hear sounds coming from the room, like something being dragged across the floor and thrown into a corner. My heart started racing again—I knew I wouldn't be able to handle another experience like I had already had that night. I admit it—I froze up and bailed out.

If I could go back in time knowing what I know now, I would have gone back in. I would have stood there until the sun came up and all through the next day just to try to have that profound contact again . . .

But I didn't. I walked out of there. I still had to mentally, emotionally, and spiritually process everything that had just gone down. For days, every time I closed my eyes, I saw the woman again. Now I understood what it means to be haunted.

Two seconds was all it took to change my life forever, two seconds that will forever be imprinted in my head. I still get goose bumps thinking about it today. It was one of the most powerful moments in my life. Whenever anybody wants to discuss my experiences in pursuit of the paranormal, this is the first story I tell. Even though I know nobody else could ever understand the magnitude of what I felt that night in those two seconds, it's the story I have to tell.

The experience in Linda Vista Hospital has helped me connect with others who have had similar encounters. Before, I couldn't really get what they were telling me, because I hadn't seen it for myself. But my experience made me a better listener to what they were trying to say, and more compassionate about why they had to say it. I now understood the compulsion to share this story. In some ways, I even understood some of the Bible stories I'd read as a kid. When you go through something that momentous, you want to stand up and tell others.

That morning, after I got back to my hotel room, I called Veronique. I described to her the whole experience exactly as it had gone down. She was blown away. "Are you serious? Holy crap!" But she understood that it had affected me on a very deep level. I also had a conversation with my dad about it. He calls me all the time to check in on me, but we'd never really had any significant discussion about some of my paranormal experiences. He usually just calls to make sure I didn't fall into a hole or something. "Dad, I know you'll never believe what happened to me," I began, and told him all about seeing the girl. When I was finished, he paused for a second, then said, "Son, I believe you."

That was a big moment for me. "Son, I believe you," my dad

had said, but to me it was validation for my career, the life I had chosen for myself. He'd always been there for me, he'd always had my back, but this was a moment of understanding. I'd never been so grateful to have him as a father.

The more this experience sank in, the more I wanted to talk about it. I started telling my family, all my friends, everyone I knew back in New England. I remember going back to my uncle Chris's house in New Hampshire a little while after the investigation. We were sitting at the bar in his house having beers with all my cousins. We were a few beers in, and Uncle Chris just looked at me and said, "So tell me . . . is it real?"

Now, in my family, there are no bullshitters. They don't mess around. I looked him right in the eyes and said, "Absolutely." I told them all about how deeply personal this experience was to me, and how it had affected me. I explained exactly what happened and exactly what I saw. And when I was done, you could tell by the looks on their faces that not one of them thought I was telling anything but the truth.

"Nick, we believe you," Uncle Chris said. "We absolutely believe you." And for the first time, those words really started to matter. I really cared if someone believed me or not.

When the Linda Vista episode aired, I felt I needed to say more than what we presented in the show. I sat down and wrote a blog about it on Facebook, something I'd never done before. But I had to share all of what I had felt, in the best way I could. If the cameras couldn't do it, maybe my words could.

A lot of fans found my reaction to seeing the girl pretty funny, because they were taking screenshots of the face I made and posting them on the Internet. But an interesting thing happened when they did that: people started to notice there's actually a mistlike anomaly that kind of forms into a hand from the right side of the frame. From Zak's angle, when he's shooting me, you can kind of see the misty figure reach into the frame and slowly try to reach for me as I jump away. Someone posted an analysis of the video, a play-by-play where you can really see the hand reach out just as my camera freezes. It turned what was already a shocking moment into a total "Holy crap!" moment. I didn't see anything like that when I watched it, not even slowing it down frame by frame. Perhaps it was because I was so intent on trying to find the girl, I didn't even see this other image.

Maybe she reached out because she wanted something from me. Maybe she wanted people to know she was there, and thought I could help her let people know. It makes you wonder. What did this spirit want? Did she need something, or did she just want me to see her? And was it to ease her mind, or my own? I think a lot about going back there, about digging through the records and the history to try to figure out who she was. Maybe that's what she wants.

I will never forget the image of this woman. I even hired an artist to sketch what I saw that night in the dark and lonely hospital.

This incredible experience would continue to affect me over the course of weeks. The eye contact was the catalyst, but the change would take some time. After Linda Vista, I feel like my eyes were opened wide to a universe of possibilities.

I've always considered myself an open-minded guy. I have been since I was a kid, including about all things paranormal—not just ghosts, but also extraterrestrials, bigfoot, and whatever else. It's not enough to just say, "Nope, that doesn't exist," and just move on. There's not enough science around just yet to know whether or not all these things are possible. That's how I look at it, and always have. And I'm not afraid to theorize a little bit either. We can't just be here purely by accident. Life can't be an anomaly of the natural world. So if we're here for a reason, then what is it?

QUESTIONS FANS ASK

How do you deal with the emotional stress of what you guys do?

I'm a pretty laid-back person, but I do sometimes get freaked out at these locations. When it's over, I remind myself that it *is* over. I calm myself down and put the experience behind me.

That's the question. Everybody starts to question why we're here at some point. It can be when you're old and beginning to fade into death, or in the immediate seconds after you've been run over by a truck. You can be a kid playing in the bathtub, or a guy just driving home from work. At some point, the question pops into your head, because it's one we spend our lives trying to answer. It's virtually impossible to know why we're alive while we're caught up in the process of actually *experiencing* it. So we hope that when we're done living, the question will be answered for us then.

That's what gets me so excited about the pursuit of the paranormal, and ghosts in particular. These people have finished living, and they may be able to share with us that big answer. We may be able to find out why we're here, without having to actually leave this plane of existence to do so. If we can perfect the science of how to communicate with the dead, we can ask the questions of why and what's next.

When I was face-to-face with that woman in Linda Vista, when she appeared to me as a solid figure, it only sparked more questions. How is this possible? How does the energy that comprises us, that supposedly dissipates when we die, come back and resurrect itself into a form we're familiar with, such as a lady standing in front of me? Is that the shape of what she knew herself to be before she died? Or is it an entity's idea of what I'd expect to see when our energies come in contact with one another?

It took two and a half years before I was ready to go back to Linda Vista for a second time. After I first saw her in July of 2009, I couldn't get her out of my mind. Who is she? What was her story? She'd changed everything about the way I approach the paranormal, and for that, I'm eternally grateful to her. I wanted to go back and do something for her.

Something else happened since the first Linda Vista episode aired. I received an interesting e-mail from a woman named Kimber Chase. Kimber was a nurse in Los Angeles in the 1980s and had to go to Linda Vista regularly to help transfer critical patients to other area hospitals. The first episode of *Ghost Adventures* that Kimber ever watched was the Linda Vista investigation.

When Kimber saw the show, she reached out to me to say that she too had seen the ghost of a young woman there, back when Linda Vista was an active hospital. She described what she saw, and it sounded a lot like the woman I saw.

The opportunity to return to Linda Vista came up in late January of 2012. We got a call telling us that in another month the building would be sold and then transformed into a convalescence home. If we wanted to investigate again, we'd have to go now. We didn't hesitate to book the trip back to East Los Angeles.

I was excited as I walked into Linda Vista for a second time. This place means so much to me. As I approached the surgical suite, I was thrilled to be there again too. I wanted to see this woman once more. I felt like I needed closure, and I wanted to tell her that it's okay to move on.

For the lockdown, I'd invited Kimber Chase to share the experience with me. When I showed Kimber the sketch I'd had drawn of the woman I saw back in 2009, she gasped. She recognized her as the same apparition she had seen back in the 1980s. We believe she was the victim of organ harvesting.

Though I didn't see this apparition on my second visit, I feel that I got what I needed. I had gone back. I spoke to the spirit of this woman and told her it was okay to move on. Whether she did or not, I don't know. But I acknowledged her, which was the most I could do for her.

On this same trip, Zak, Aaron, and I decided to visit the LA coroner's office, the largest of its kind in the United States, and not far from Linda Vista. It was an experience I'll never forget.

The coroner hit a button and a large metal door slid open. Inside were 289 bodies covered in white sheets. The smell took my breath away. It was like formaldehyde combined with the most pungent rot I've ever smelled. The three of us took turns walking in there alone holding a camera.

The room is cold: thirty-seven degrees, to be precise. Just enough to slow down decomposition.

As I walk in, I'm okay for the moment. I see bullet holes in one guy. I see a woman's foot that looks like it melted in a fire. I see an obese man splayed out on a table, and another man with half his head missing. Then I start to see their faces and it hits me that these were living people. That energy that makes us human was there and now is gone. All of us are destined to end up like this.

It's powerful when you walk in the valley of death like that.

Before Linda Vista, I was on this quest because I was a believer—just an inexperienced believer. In that dark hospital ward, my beliefs became validated.

That moment in July of 2009 was like the first chapter of my new life. I couldn't wait to see what happened next.

CHAPTER 14

MY PARANORMAL LIFE

Some people might look at what I've accomplished and say, "Dude, you've made it." I played a big part in making a popular documentary that aired on national television and helped create a very popular television series. I've been on *Maury* and the *Howard Stern Show*, been interviewed on countless TV news stations, and been profiled in magazine and newspaper articles.

But that's what I've been able to accomplish in the entertainment field, and I don't think I ever "made it." That makes it sound like it was an overnight thing, as if somebody handed us a television show and we became an instant success. "Made it" also sounds like I have nothing left to accomplish—and I know that's far from true.

I've worked hard over the years to get to this point. Everything was a building block, a stepping-stone, and it wasn't until season five of *Ghost Adventures* that I stopped looking over my shoulder or waiting for the other shoe to drop. During season five, I felt like I could get back to some of my other passions: music, screenplays, and other television show ideas.

The weird dichotomy of making this show is that we're actually serving two masters: the television viewers and the paranormal community. They're not mutually exclusive, of course, but there's a difference in what we owe each one. If *Ghost Adventures* ever stops being interesting to people or generating ratings and advertising dollars, it will be canceled. That's pretty straightforward, and we knew that was part of the whole package going in. But the other side of it is the place we've carved out for ourselves as paranormal investigators. For better or worse and certainly not through our own doing, we're considered leaders in the field and innovators for the approach and the equipment we use. That wasn't our intention; we just wanted to conduct the best investigations we could, and that meant being cutting-edge in technology, technique, and theory.

QUESTIONS FANS ASK

Does your wife believe in ghosts? Have any ever followed you home and scared your family?

Veronique does believe in ghosts and has since she was a child. Her father passed away when she was one, and she's been very spiritual ever since. She had a bad experience with a Ouija board as a teenager when she watched the planchette move across the board without anyone touching it, and she believes she had an encounter with my grandma Groff right after she died. When my grandma died, I was filming the *Ghost Adventures* documentary at the Washoe Club. Veronique woke up that night back in our home in Las Vegas to the feeling of someone wiggling her big toe. She felt like it was my grandma's spirit coming to let her know that she was okay and I was okay at the Washoe Club.

As for something following me home, there was one time I had just finished filming a location right before Halloween. When I got home, my cousin Justin had come to stay with us for a couple of days. I bought a Halloween mask and took a picture of it. In the photo I saw a strange ball of energy near it. We all saw it. Like an idiot, I ran to grab my audio recorder to do an EVP session.

In the playback we heard three different voices: a little kid's voice, an old lady's voice, and this growl. We were all freaked out when we went to bed that night. But the EVP wasn't the end of the experience. Around two in the morning I heard pots and pans banging around in my kitchen and the sound of the sink filling up with water. I was sure there was a burglar in my house. I got up and pushed my two dogs, Coco, an English springer spaniel, and Scrappy Doo, a Yorkie, out into the hall. The dogs were just as freaked out as the rest of us. Then the sounds stopped. Ever since then I don't investigate or do any EVP sessions in my house anymore. I love my work, but I don't want to take it home!

I'm still finding my way in the paranormal field. There's so much we don't know, you can never be comfortable enough with what you do know. No matter what you believe, something can come along in an instant—like the spirit I saw in Linda Vista—that shatters all your preconceived notions. It's not the paranormal that's evolving, but our understanding of the paranormal.

It's always bothered me that when you think the paranormal exists, it's called belief and subject to ridicule and mockery. But when you buy into religion unabashedly, it's called faith, and that's perfectly acceptable. "Belief" is a word that has grown to have almost negative connotations. But "faith"—well, faith is all right, as long as it doesn't step on someone else's faith at the same time.

Lots of people believe in the existence of the paranormal, and especially ghosts, but they're operating on faith. It's different once you've had that faith rewarded by verifiable proof, and that's something not everybody gets to experience. I will always consider myself lucky that I did.

Since my Linda Vista experience, my life has accelerated. I've grown as a person, I've grown spiritually, and my family has grown as well. Veronique and I always knew we wanted to have a family. It was only about six months after Linda Vista that Veronique got pregnant. Once that encounter had soaked into me, I got a healthy reminder of what's really important: my family, my wife, my friends, and living.

My daughter, Annabelle, was born on December 7, 2010, at seven a.m. I was right there for her birth. It's nerve-racking to be at your wife's side when she is in labor, but there's not much I could do except be supportive. But there was a single moment, just a few seconds after Annabelle was born, that something forced me through a flood of emotions.

Two seconds . . .

. . . I heard my daughter's first cry.

Every single emotion poured out of me at once. Joy, pain, laughter, sorrow at the thought of family members who were no longer around to see this perfect little girl—all of it came out. A switch was thrown inside of me. I'm Annabelle's dad now. Now I am fully alive and awake.

Putting this into words is so difficult for me. It's like the paranormal—until you actually experience it, it's hard to comprehend. Anyone who is a parent can understand. Annabelle's birth completed my transformation. I understood that part of my place in this world would be to provide for her and love her unconditionally. She's counting on me, and I will be there for her forever.

I had to leave for the next *Ghost Adventures* shoot just four days after Annabelle was born. That was really difficult—it was our Jerome, Arizona, episode. It's ironic that it was there that I could sleep for the first time in four days!

As sleep deprived as I was, I've never felt so spiritually strong as I did in the months following Annabelle's birth.

Although some religious zealots might disagree, the principles of faith that allow some people to believe in ghosts are the same ones that allow others to believe in heaven. It's all about believing that there's more to life than just what we experience in this plane of existence, and that there's something more to death than just a fade to black. It all boils down to the same question: what's next?

That thought is never too far from my mind. In fact, I thought about it to the point where I started writing some lyrics to a song I was kicking around in my head. It's called "What's Next?" Using music, I could explore how I feel after all that I've been through. What is next? Do we die and just go into the ground, our consciousness extinguished as our bodies turn to dust? I don't see how that's possible, since I know energy doesn't die. The energy lives on. So does it travel through another dimension, or does it linger in this dimension in which we live our lives? Maybe the Buddhists are right, and energy is reincarnated into a new physical form. But then again, maybe that energy travels through a wormhole into some other, alternate dimension, where our same self is reborn.

Music has been a part of my life since childhood. To be a good filmmaker, I need to understand how music can express emotions that aren't always said by the people on-screen or expressed in the visuals. Music can make you uncomfortable in a *good* way at the right moment. If someone is lurking down the hall and you know the killer is just around the corner, some tense string instruments can feel like knuckles running up your spine. Though I put my focus on filmmaking and television, I've never forgotten about music.

Through Facebook, I was able to reconnect with my childhood friend Danny Bedrosian, the musical master now rocking with George Clinton and his band. He and I had been talking for the last couple of years about making music again—it's been a long time since our band, Dysfunctional Family, played at a school dance. It was fun to reminisce, but then I realized how much I missed having that creative outlet in my life. During the summer of 2011, I was writing tons of lyrics and jotting down song ideas

QUESTIONS FANS ASK

Do you think ghost hunting puts your soul in danger? Do you think doing this kind of work will determine whether you go to heaven or to hell?

I don't know what's going to happen to me. I don't know if there is a heaven or hell. But either way I'd like to think I'll be judged on my actions, not on my investigations.

I've always had a higher power in my life. I've prayed for guidance when times are hard, and I've even reached out to the spirit of my grandmother who passed away years ago. I ask God to help me get through the tough times. After a difficult investigation I often pray for guidance and protection.

beyond just "What's Next?" Then, in the fall, the two of us got together in Tallahassee, Florida, to start putting down the tracks.

When I started writing music again, I had no agenda or plan. But when you create something artistic, you have to go with what you know. Looking for ghosts and trekking through haunted places is a huge part of who I am now. I didn't mean to, but I found myself writing music about the big questions the paranormal brought up inside of me. Death, life, afterlife, what it all means. Evil, good—all those things were swirling around in my head.

I've found a lot of meaning in my life through the paranormal, and that came out in my music. Here are the lyrics to one of the songs on my album, *The Other Side*.

Life

Courtesy of Groff Entertainment, LLC (BMI)/ Bozfonk Moosick (BMI) © 2011. All rights reserved.

You have one life, what will you do with it? This is the only way to express mine:

You ever look death in the eyes, feel the misery pass and watch your loved one die? I have, the worst part has passed, I'm up next, I can feel the wrath approach with a swift taste from his ash.

FUCK THAT, I don't want to die yet, Annabelle needs a father figure to help her grow, to reach the stars, stars need to form from energy and I'm her heart.

The future is born with one rhythmic beat apart. I'll take death and strangle him before he takes me.

(CHORUS)

Life is so sudden, Life is so instant. You better take your Life and not get it twisted. Dying is the easy part, Living is the hard part, some are forgotten and some live on . . .

. . . on and on till that last song, ears are ringing, as the heart is gone . . . FLAT-LINE . . .

I began to drift, with an emotional kiss, Memories evaporate, no more tears as energy escapes, the capsule is lost, time fucking stops, Life is a blink of an eye away, Darkness erupts, motherfuckers clutch, Sin is tough—the route of all evil, you made the most outta being the host, but there's complications, so swallow your fear on this explanation, to the eternal mark on your God-willing part . . .

(CHORUS)

Life is so sudden, Life is so instant. You better take your Life and not get it twisted. Dying is the easy part, Living is the hard part, some are forgotten and some live on . . .

These are the thoughts that go through my head. I am by no means trying to make you buy into one belief or another—what you believe is your own business, and I respect whatever choices you make—but we must remain open-minded to the many possibilities. Science cannot prove or disprove what happens to us after we die. And to be honest, neither can religion. Perhaps the paranormal field is the closest we can get to finding that answer, and even that is a long way off.

The Other Side is all about overcoming obstacles, and I wanted to put in as much positivity as I could. I know some folks will buy the music just because they're *Ghost Adventures* fans. That's cool, but it gives me an opportunity to get a message across too.

I realize my position now is to bring awareness more than anything, rather than manipulate people into buying into any set of beliefs. Follow your own faith; I'm no prophet. Nobody in the paranormal field is. I still can't figure out why I'm on this earth, why I was born into this life in particular. We all like to think we have some kind of destiny, some greater importance to our existence, but think about it: in the grand scheme of things, just how significant are our lives? We live for a blink in a cosmic eye, where fifty or a hundred years is but a nanosecond.

I want to live my life as an open book. Out on the road I meet so many people who are interested in what I do. Even skeptics, the ones who actually do keep an open mind, have to raise an eyebrow at some of the experiences that I share with them.

Some religions don't strictly adhere to the heaven-or-hell theory after we die. To some, there's an in-between. In Catholicism, it's called purgatory. Purgatory is a place of purification for souls who are destined for heaven but haven't quite lived up to the purification required to go through the gates. Some feel that ghosts exist in this state of purgatory, still in the process of earning their way into heaven. Others believe that our existence itself may be purgatory, that we're in between heaven and hell and this is the limbo we're stuck with.

As for me, ever since I had the experience at Linda Vista, I've wondered if maybe this isn't my own purgatory, my chance at spiritual growth and enlightenment. That one moment—two seconds—woke me up. It made me want to live life in a big way, and that includes connecting with more people in every way.

My paranormal experiences have made me less combative with skeptics, believe it or not. Whenever I do radio interviews or convention appearances, someone inevitably will ask me, "What do you say to skeptics?" The answer is I don't say any-thing, really. It's not my job to make them believe, just as they shouldn't feel it's their job to make me *not* believe. Everyone has their own views; everybody has to live their own life, have their own experiences, and go through their own journey or destiny that will take them to what's next. This is my life and these are my experiences, and all I can do is talk about them and let people know. If it opens up someone's mind a little more so that they can perhaps have their own experience, that's a bonus.

The word "skeptic" is often misused, because so many skeptics—especially those who make their living off it—aren't skeptical about the existence of the paranormal. They're outright nonbelievers, and nothing is going to change their mind. They're out there telling people things that science hasn't even been able to prove or disprove yet—just as we are—but for some reason they're sure that they're right and I'm wrong. It can't work that way, guys. Too many so-called skeptics are starting to sound like those religious zealots who say that their way is the only way, and anybody who says otherwise is speaking the words of the devil.

Some cry out for empirical proof, data that can be repeated

again and again in a laboratory setting. Here's the problem with that: it's not the labs that are haunted. For reasons we can't quite figure out yet, these energies are only able to manifest in certain locations. Once we do, maybe then we can re-create them in the lab. For now, we have to bring the lab to them, which is what we're trying to do with repeated paranormal investigation of these locations. And even then, we can lay out all the geophysical information, atmospheric readings, and EMF fluctuations in the world, but that still won't explain why I saw a solid figure of a woman appear right before my very eyes, where a split second before there was nothing but darkness. There's no meter or detector that's been created that can measure that . . . yet. So instead, these skeptics go with the old standby that it's "just in your mind."

The mind is an interesting thing. It's said that we use only 10 or 15 percent of it. The skeptics believe it's that 10 or 15 percent that is mistaken about what I saw, but what if instead it's the unknown 85 to 90 percent that might actually perceive it?

That's why the paranormal is such an interesting frontier, and maybe one of the last left to explore. Nobody can speak hard and fast about it, because nothing is certain or proven. It's all theory. I've been doing this for a while now, and I've been to all kinds of haunted locations all over the world. I've had tons of experiences in those places, and I'd like to think I can determine when my eyes are playing tricks on me and when I'm seeing something that is real. I have no problem admitting that, sometimes, that just might be the case—hey, it's dark, and I'm using just a little LCD screen as my light source. It's easy to mistake shadows out of the corner of your eye for something else.

But I also know that when I turn around and see a freaking

person standing there, and it scares the ever living crap out of me and changes my life forever, it's not my mind playing tricks on me! I would have known the difference even then. And it's insulting that "skeptics" would think otherwise.

QUESTIONS FANS ASK

When are you going to start your own show?

Ghost Adventures is just one piece of who I am and what I do. I'm working on other projects all the time. I recently helped create a new television series for the Travel Channel called *Vegas Stripped*. I'm not on camera for that show, but I love the idea. Plus, I'm working on other paranormal show ideas where I would be on camera exploring all kinds of strange legends.

I'm not sure exactly what happens when we die, but I like to think that I'm not going to stick around. I'd like to go to a different place, to a different challenge. Whatever is next, I'm ready for it.

Thinking about myself as a ghost also makes me question how I'd feel if I were one of the spirits that we're investigating for *Ghost Adventures*. I mean, were I to die and Zak showed up trying to make contact with my spirit, I'd haunt the shit out of him and everyone involved! Zak thinks three scratches down his back at Bobby Mackey's is something? I'd make his head go all the way around! (Think of the ratings, Zak!)

I look at it like this: if I were wandering through some sort of limbo and unable to communicate with anyone, and then some people showed up and attempted to make contact with me, I don't think I'd be upset. I don't know exactly what I would feel, but I don't think it would be anger.

The paranormal is always at my core, but I'm still a storyteller and sometimes other stories are going to call out to me. In 2011, I got serious about pitching other television series ideas—some paranormal, some not. Because *Ghost Adventures* has been successful and I'm an executive producer on that show, it's easy for me to get an audience with television production companies and networks now.

Vegas Stripped is one of my recent projects, and it was picked up by the Travel Channel in November of 2011. Living in Las Vegas for so many years, I got the chance to know some of the casinos and their owners. I have a neighbor who is a real old-school Vegas guy—he used to work in Bugsy Siegel's hotel when he was young. This neighbor introduced me to the owners of the South Point Casino, one of the newer and very popular casino hotels in town. After speaking with the owners and some of their management, I knew there was a great concept for a show there. The idea was to follow a day in the life of casino security.

The South Point Casino was willing to open up its security cameras to a television series so we could witness the everyday employee work atmosphere, events, and human drama that unfold on a daily basis in a major Vegas casino. How cool is that?

But putting something like this together is tricky. The casino doesn't want to make itself look bad, and of course we need to show the juicy stuff if people are going to watch. That's one thing I respected South Point for in a big way. These guys were willing to bare it all. They figured that by showing how well they handled security situations, in the end they'd look even better.

I loved the whole process. And the Travel Channel loved it too. The show started airing in February 2012.

Even though I already had a hit show to my name, I still had to do a lot of work to get *Vegas Stripped* sold. First of all, I'd had to work that connection with my neighbor to make my pitch to the casino. Then I had to develop the idea, invest my own money to get the sizzle reel produced, and shop it around. If the show didn't sell, I'd be out all that money and time. But I believed in this idea. I knew it would be fun to watch and fun to make. I had to see it through.

I'm so fortunate to be in a position to turn my creative ideas into reality. And I'm working on other projects too. I'm drawn to human interest stories where people overcome obstacles. I love cheering for folks in rough situations.

Since working on *Ghost Adventures*, I also grew into my own sense of style. After I'd made my documentary, I'd realized how dorky I looked in the clothes I wore and made some changes to my wardrobe. So when a clothing designer called Modus Collections approached me about creating my own clothing line, I jumped at the chance.

In the past, Zak and I had sold Ghost Adventures Crew T-shirts and sweatshirts. The problem was, it was difficult to manage the inventory—I had to fulfill the orders and get them to the post office. We did all that ourselves. With traveling and everything else, we couldn't keep up with it, so we stopped. I was blown away by how supportive our fans were—they even wanted to wear our clothing.

I've come to realize that the three of us—Zak, Aaron, and myself—represent a lifestyle and a mood. We're the guys on television who aren't afraid to go into the darkest haunts on the planet.

Maybe by emulating us just a bit, people get to break out of their daily lives and feel more a part of the Ghost Adventures Crew.

Working with Modus Collections allowed me to reconnect with JoAnne DeOleo, an old friend from high school who helped me put together my Phantom Collection line of clothes. One area that's been tough for me since the success of *Ghost Adventures* is trusting people. Working with old friends makes that easier.

My wife knows me better than anyone, and she took the lead on the designs and worked with JoAnne to create exactly what I wanted. Veronique has been there for everything, so she was able to take my ideas and my life and turn them into a look. One of my favorite designs she came up with is a dark hoodie with the song lyrics from my song "Black Death" in the shape of a G. Another design features a ghostly doctor. Another favorite is called "1862." The artwork was inspired by some of the architecture from Virginia City, and 1862 was the year some of my favorite buildings in town were constructed. I feel such a connection to that town it inspires almost every part of my life.

I wear my Phantom Collection clothes on a regular basis. The line launched on Halloween 2011 and has been well received so far. I plan to introduce more designs and clothes as time goes on.

From attending *Ghost Adventures* events and meeting fans all over the place, I'm humbled and amazed by how much they want to be a part of what we do. We're kind of like a subculture—a group of friends out to explore the unexplained, and if people want to join us for the ride, then they're welcome to.

I know the clothes, the music, and even this book may look like I'm trying to cash in on something, but the reality is I don't do something unless my heart is in it 100 percent. When you work in a creative field, you can't fake it. If you make art that is half-assed, people will see through it. People aren't stupid. They recognize when something is genuine. Real art is about telling the truth to your audience.

That honesty is something I try to convey in every episode of *Ghost Adventures*, and in everything I put out to the public.

I want to be a positive force for change. I'm in a position where I can do that. And so is everyone else. I truly believe any obstacle can be overcome. I'm just getting started.

CHAPTER 15

THE SPIRITUAL JOURNEY

It's taken a long time for my mind and spirit to accept that there's something else out there after we die. I feel that this is something I've always known, but I needed to prove it to myself to be 100 percent certain. Looking for ghosts and, in particular, that experience at Linda Vista Hospital accomplished that.

I think of my life now as a continual transformation. I'm evolving because of my experiences. Sometimes that evolution takes leaps—like when I locked eyes with a spirit—but most of the time that change occurs in tiny steps that are too small to notice. But over time they add up.

I've learned a lot along the way about the filmmaking craft and about paranormal investigating. But above all, I've learned about myself. I know enough to know there's plenty more to learn—I take a lot of comfort in that.

I was asked recently by my old UNLV professor Francisco Menendez to come back and speak to the film department. So I started thinking about what I would say to the students. What would I say to a younger version of me if I could?

I knew I'd ask the students: "How many of you want to be filmmakers?" I imagined I'd see just about every hand in the auditorium go up—that's how it was when I was in school. My follow-up question would be: "What are you going to do about it?"

Sure, they're in school to learn about the process and the business. That's a good start. And I imagined they would have been attending my lecture to get the answer to my second question. But here's the thing: I don't know what *they* should do about it. I just know what *I* did about it.

Going to school doesn't move you any closer to actually *being* a filmmaker. A filmmaker captures stories and finds a unique and captivating way to tell them. You can learn about cameras, editing, pitching ideas, and all that other stuff in school. But you must have the heart of a filmmaker. And you must do things for yourself. A filmmaker is a doer, a problem solver. You don't have the money? Find it. You don't have the cameras? Borrow one, buy one, or rent one. You don't have an actor? What about that guy who made your sandwich at the deli yesterday? He was a real character and would be perfect. Ask him! Start filming and start editing. That's the only way to get better. That's how I got to where I am today, and that's how every filmmaker I know got to where he or she is today. If you need your hand held every step of the way, filmmaking isn't for you.

I also get asked for a lot of advice when it comes to paranormal investigation. People see me do this on television and they want to try it for themselves. I recommend people find a local paranormal investigation group to get started—they're all over the place. Search online, or attend paranormal events in your region. An established group can show you the ropes, but that

QUESTIONS FANS ASK

Would you ever want to own a haunted building?

Yes. I would love to own Linda Vista Hospital in Los Angeles. That building still haunts me. If I owned it I could turn it into a kind of paranormal laboratory. The only problem is it would cost millions, and so far my lottery tickets aren't covering it.

alone isn't enough. Learn all you can on your own. Read books, but not just paranormal books—read what the skeptics have to say, read books on science and energy. Exploring the paranormal is all about testing your own theories. It's a journey.

One of the strangest questions I get is from people who think the paranormal is an easy way to get on television. They want to know how their group can get their own show. I try to be helpful, but I question the motive. You should be in the paranormal world because you're passionate about the work and the study. If you get into it for any other reason, viewers (and television executives long before the viewers) will see right through you.

Whatever you do in life, follow your passion. If you want to be on TV, be an actor. If you want to pursue the paranormal, do it! If you're innovative, if your passion for the subject comes through, you may end up on TV—who knows? But the goal should always be to do what you love. When you go looking for ghosts week after week, death becomes your business. What happens after we die becomes an ever present thought. I want to be remembered for who I am and what I did after I'm gone. I want to be someone people could look up to. It's easy for an asshole to be remembered—those guys stand out. But to be remembered for being someone positive—that takes something more. *That's* what I work toward.

I've had the chance to talk with religious people of all persuasions, and one thing I've noticed is that no two people will agree on what happens in the afterlife. Even married couples who've attended the same church for decades will have different ideas on the afterlife.

QUESTIONS FANS ASK

How do you keep your cool during tense moments in an investigation?

You do get used to being in these frightening locations and situations. Once you've faced the paranormal down a few times, you know what to expect—not that I still don't get surprised on occasion. It's similar to people who hunt dangerous animals. It's good to have a healthy amount of fear to keep you sharp, but if you're not ready to face that fear, then paranormal investigation is not for you.

From childhood I've been thinking deep thoughts about all aspects of the unknown. Even in the Bible there's a description of a spaceship. In the book of Ezekiel, chapter one describes in great detail the technology of a wheel-within-a-wheel craft that comes down from the heavens with multiple humanoid entities on board. The description isn't spiritual, it's technical.

What if some of these UFOs we're seeing are ourselves time traveling from the future? What if some of these ghosts are us catching a glimpse of the past? There's so much that isn't known out there. That's what draws me in. I want to know. I have big questions, and I'm inviting everyone along for the ride as I search for answers.

Nothing is impossible. Not so long ago, people thought it was impossible to fly to the moon. But we did that in 1969. So many "impossibilities" have become commonplace that it almost seems ridiculous to call anything impossible anymore. Yet some still do. It's not true. We're limited only by our imaginations. The paranormal *will* be proven, even if it's to one person at a time.

Through my ghost investigations, I've become more spiritual and less religious. That might sound like a cop-out, but it's not. I still pray, I reach out to my grandmothers almost daily for help and guidance, and I constantly think about what positive change I can make on my life and the people around me. There are still bad days, of course. Some days I have lawyers calling, projects stalling, or issues with people I work with, but still I push through. I try to stay more positive than negative because in the end I know I'm winning more than I'm losing.

Life is short. Working in television, and especially my return to music, has helped me realize I'm here for a reason. I've been through the highs and the lows. I get it.

I turned my passion into my career. I keep my love for doing this because I'm still an adrenaline junkie. I still find it thrilling to explore haunted locations and see what we turn up. I want to have more experiences like I did at Linda Vista. I'll be ready for it next time. If the entity reaches out to me, I'll want to reach back. I'll ask: "What is it like where you are?"

In many respects, I feel like spirits are calling out to me to keep doing this. That's fine—I have no plans to stop. Through doing this I can be an example to others.

Working on *Ghost Adventures* and living in the public eye have made me more confident in who I am. I recently did a live interview on a morning show in Las Vegas. I sat down in their studio and talked about the show and my experiences with ghosts. When it was over, I walked out of the studio thinking, *How cool is that?* First, that someone would find me newsworthy, and second, that I wasn't nervous at all. Live TV—who knows how many people are watching at home?—and I'm completely comfortable in my own skin. I know who I am, I know what I have experienced, and I'm happy to tell others about it—whether it's to someone standing next to me or in front of a television audience.

I realize I'm blessed. Some people live their entire lives without ever getting comfortable or even knowing who they are. I still have more to learn—I know this. But I know who I am right now. I know the journey I'm on is spiritual, and it always has been.

I'm Nick Groff. I'm a filmmaker. I'm a paranormal investigator. I'm a musician. I'm an author. I'm a dad. I'm a husband. I'm a son and a brother. And I believe in ghosts!

PARANORMAL INVESTIGATION
EQUIPMENT

THERMAL IMAGING CAMERA: If you've seen the *Predator* movie series starring Arnold Schwarzenegger, then you have a sense of what a thermal imaging camera sees: heat, or more specifically, infrared radiation. By looking for infrared energy, the camera can create a video picture in which warmer temperatures show up as light colors or white and cooler temperatures show up as dark blues and purples. The FLIR camera I use can give you a scale of temperature ranges in its field of vision accurate up to one hundredth of a degree. It can detect temperatures between −4°F and 482°F and then create a rainbow-colored video image. It looks amazing—and it had better, considering how much these things cost! They can range from a few thousand to over fifteen thousand bucks.

This piece of equipment was designed for military, law enforcement, and emergency workers and later adapted by electricians and contractors to look for heat signatures inside of buildings. Emergency workers can use them to look through walls for warm bodies who may be unconscious; contractors can look through walls to wires and pipes that might be glowing hot and in need of fixing.

As with a lot of equipment paranormal investigators use, we have taken this tool and adapted it for what we do. I use a thermal camera to look for spirit energy. If there are cold spots or hot spots in a room, this camera finds them. Sometimes I may see a warm, misty figure floating in the room through the camera and then quickly learn that its source is a heat vent right below—no ghost, but at least I know. Then there are times when I see something on the camera that looks exactly like a human figure. When I see the bright colors of a human body, my first thought is that there's a person nearby—maybe someone I'm investigating with, or someone who maybe shouldn't be where I am right now. Usually there's a normal explanation for what this camera picks up, but once in a while there isn't.

I used this camera while investigating outside the Gettysburg Engine House in Pennsylvania. This was the exact spot where the Battle of Gettysburg began back on July 1, 1863. We aimed the camera down the railroad tracks and captured a human shape walking. The shape was dark blue, meaning the camera detected this figure as colder than the environment. When I looked ahead, I saw nothing with my naked eye. That's when my heart started racing. This piece of equipment doesn't know how to fake evidence. It just looks for temperatures and displays what it sees. Could it be that this camera saw a Civil War spirit that was pulling energy out of the environment and creating an area colder than everything else around it? Let me put it this way: if that isn't what happened, then I can't explain what I saw on the thermal camera any other way.

EM PUMP: One theory about ghosts and spirits is that either they are made up of electromagnetic energy or they use electromagnetic energy to make things happen in our world. So creating a cold spot may draw a small amount of energy from the room, while pushing a living person into a wall most likely takes a lot of energy. This may explain why the batteries we use sometimes suddenly drain for no apparent reason. The EM pump was invented by Bill Chappell, an engineer, inventor, and ghost investigator who builds this stuff to test paranormal theories. The EM pump was designed to give spirits a beacon to follow.

According to Bill, the device creates a small electromagnetic field around it that changes in frequency from .2 to 256 Hz. It makes a kind of electromagnetic white noise, similar to when you hear a police siren behind you on the highway. That sound goes low to high, back and forth—it's designed to get your attention. Same with the EM pump. "If I put something in the room that makes this obnoxious noise," Bill explained, "sooner or later you're going to go look for it."

When I place one of these devices in paranormal hot spots, more activity seems to happen. I get more electronic voice phenomena and I hear more unexplained noises. So this beacon is definitely doing something to attract spirit activity.

EMF METER: An EMF meter or detector measures electromagnetic fields. The theory is that spirits are either made up of electromagnetic energy, or manipulate those fields in order to do something like make a sound, materialize, or move objects. If that's true, then an EMF meter should measure some kind of fluctuation. There are many different brands and types of meters. I'll go through some of those below.

TRIFIELD METER: This device is also known as a natural electromagnetic meter because it's designed to detect only DC, or direct current, that mostly comes from natural electric and magnetic sources like the earth's magnetic field, high solar activity, static electricity, and nearby thunderstorms. The electricity in your house runs on AC, or alternating current, but the Trifield meter isn't looking for those frequencies. It's called "Trifield" because it measures in three directions: the X, Y, and Z axes. The device can even detect electromagnetic activity in living people—some people carry an electronic charge, though others do not.

If spirits are moving the natural electromagnetic fields of a room, the needle on this device will move to show how strong the force is. It also has a buzzer alarm on it so you can set it down and leave it alone like an electromagnetic motion detector. If you hear the buzzer, that means some electromagnetic field has just come into contact with the device. It doesn't necessarily mean a ghost, but it does mean some force has moved through the room.

I know that's getting technical, so here's what the Trifield meter basically means to me: if I'm sensing something weird in a haunted location, like a tingling sensation or a cold spot, or if I'm hearing strange sounds in the room, I pull out this meter. If it picks something up, that's just one more piece of evidence of a paranormal event.

DIGITAL AUDIO RECORDER: An EVP, or electronic voice phenomenon, is one of the most compelling pieces of paranormal evidence out there. When I'm holding my recorder and asking questions, then play it back and hear a response to my question that I didn't hear before—whoa, that's big. There are tons of audio recorders out there that people use for EVP. Some people like to buy analog recorders with microcassettes; others, like myself, use a digital recorder—it's easier to work with the sound files later and analyze them by computer.

Making contact through EVP is a simple process, but it still takes practice and some work. When I'm getting ready, I try to clear my head and think about the location I'm in. I try to ask questions that make sense to the spirits believed to be there. If I'm in a former Civil War field hospital, I won't be asking about aircraft fire or machine guns. I want to get my mind into the right time period. I know these ghosts are around me somewhere, and I try to talk to them the same way I'd talk to a living person I haven't met yet.

You have to think about how weird you might look to a spirit on the other side. There you are in strange clothes, holding some little device with a red light on it—you look completely out of place. When I do an EVP session, I start my recorder, introduce myself, and tell the surrounding spirits that this little machine won't hurt them, but it may be able to record their voice so we can talk to each other. Then I ask a few questions that relate to the time period or location. I'll ask their name, how old they are. I may turn it up a bit and ask who attacked them, for instance, if I know a murder took place where I'm standing. You need to leave a few seconds between questions for the answers to come through.

Something else you need to do is "tag" normal sounds. So if I've just asked a question and a loud truck rolls by outside a second later, I'll announce in a normal voice, "A truck just drove by." If you're not reviewing the audio evidence until days or weeks later, you might forget that a truck drove by at that moment and think you've picked up a demonic growl instead.

I try to keep my EVP sessions short—maybe two or three minutes at most, so I can play them back right away while I'm standing there. If I get a voice, I can try to keep the conversation going, or break out more gear, like an EMF meter, an electronic device we use to measure the amount of electromagnetic energy in the area.

My audio recorder of choice is the Olympus 4100PC digital recorder, which has been working great for me since the beginning. I recall seeing one investigator doing an EVP session where he literally laid out six different audio recorders—different brands and models. Then he'd ask questions and review all of that audio later. If a response is picked up on one recorder but not another, that's really interesting. And I can tell you that happens. Sometimes my recorder will pick up responses that others' in the same room do not.

EVP is amazing when you get results. The first few times I tried it, I got nothing. But the more you work with it, the more you start to pick up voices.

OVILUS II: The Ovilus is another Bill Chappell invention, and it's sometimes a controversial one in the paranormal community. I never thought much about the device until I was working on this book and figured people might want to know the story behind it. So I called Bill. First, the name: "It roughly means 'the great one' in Greek," Chappell said. The idea started back in 2005 when Bill watched a ghost investigator trying to communicate with spirits by using dowsing rods, or metal rods bent into an L-shape and held in each hand. The rods would cross to indicate "yes," and spread apart for "no." Bill thought that looked a bit unscientific, so he wondered if he could improve on the concept.

The idea of dowsing goes back thousands of years. People have used forked sticks, bent wires, and weighted objects at the end of chains or strings to try to focus their intent on what they're looking for.

Bill is an engineer by trade and knew that there are electromagnetic forces moving around us all the time. If those forces could move bent wires, then he could build something to measure the response. His first "digital dowsing rods" were a machine with two rows of LED lights running down each side. If the electromagnetic force favored the right side, then those lights lit up showing the strength of the force. If it came from the left, then lights to the left lit up.

Chappell took that digital dowsing a step further. He developed a system that would measure when the environment changes. What kind of changes? Bill said, "I'm looking for when the environment changes in either electromagnetic force, ionization, static electricity, or capacitive fields." Translation: when energy moves or gets stronger or weaker in a given place, Bill's machine measures the change to get a result. Based on the result, the Ovilus II will speak either a word or phonetic sound (depending on which setting you select), and speak it. It's believed that spirits can manipulate the environment to get a message across using this device.

I know this sounds complicated, but hang in there for a minute. If I'm holding the Ovilus II in an old mental hospital in a ward where a doctor was once arrested for torturing patients, and I ask a question like, "Who hurt you?" and the Ovilus II says, "Doctor," then a few seconds later says, "hurt," then a second later says, "knife," what are the odds that those responses are due to random chance? When you add up these remote chances, the evidence becomes compelling. And if we can combine interesting Ovilus data with temperature fluctuations or personal experiences such as hearing voices or seeing an apparition, then I'm very interested in what's going on at that location.

PX: The PX is another Bill Chappell device, but this one has a few extras. Bill explained that he was tired of people dissing the name Ovilus, so it was one part name change and another part better technology. The PX is more sensitive than the Ovilus; it's smaller and it has outputs so we can plug it into a display, like our heads-up goggles or a video feed, while we use it. There's no confusion over what has been said with the PX, because you also see the word the dictionary just spit out; plus the software will put a time stamp on each word as it's said, so you know exactly when each word was said during the investigation.

The number one question Bill gets about the PX and the Ovilus is, "Can it hear what you're saying?" The answer is no. It's not equipped with a microphone and doesn't have the capacity to process what was said anyway. Bill does believe that our subconscious mind might be able to affect the device—which would still be amazing!

PUCK: Also developed by Bill Chappell, the Puck was launched in 2006, and was meant to give investigators total control over what the device is looking for. It's similar to the Ovilus and PX, but the Puck has the ability to move its sensitivity and scale through software. "If you're in a room with a bunch of devices operating at 60 Hz," Bill explained, "you can tell the Puck to ignore 60 Hz and only look at higher frequencies." He stopped making the Puck because a lot of people found it too complicated to use. On *Ghost Adventures* we still bring ours out to investigations, though, because you never know what device is going to work where.

MEL-8704 METER: We use the Mel meter a lot on *Ghost Adventures* because it shows us an EMF reading and a temperature reading at the same time and in one device. The Mel-8704 meter was developed by electronics engineer Gary Galka. The story behind the meter is touching and personal—its history is quite different from any other piece of equipment out there.

Gary's daughter Melissa was born on Valentine's Day in 1987. One night in late September of 2004, she was out for the evening. Her curfew was twelve thirty. "Around twelve fifteen, I got up and I felt something was wrong," Galka said. "So I got up, got dressed, and went to the front bay window and was looking out. I felt something in my gut . . . something wasn't right. All of a sudden I see car headlights coming down the street and then up our driveway and I'm thinking, *Thank God, she's home.* But then the doorbell started ringing frantically, so I ran downstairs and one of Mel's good friends said Melissa was in front of her and she saw Melissa run off the road and hit a tree."

A parent's worst nightmare was coming true. Galka jumped into the car and raced the two minutes down the road to the accident scene. Later police would estimate that Melissa had hit the tree going sixty miles per hour. The car's engine was pushed right up to the dashboard, and it wasn't possible to get Melissa out of the car when Gary first arrived.

"I held her hand through the broken window and talked to her," Gary said. "Even though she was unconscious, she was moaning." Gary figured she could hear his words.

No one knows exactly what happened to Melissa to distract her from driving. She was alone in her car and following her boyfriend, who was driving very fast. Maybe an animal jumped into the road; maybe it was something else. The Galka family will never know.

Rescuers used the Jaws of Life to cut the metal around

Melissa so they could remove her from the car and rush her to the hospital. During the ambulance ride Melissa regained consciousness and was able to tell the EMTs her name and date of birth. Hopes were high that Melissa would recover, but after four days in the intensive care unit, doctors determined her brain had suffered too much trauma and she would not survive. The Galkas had to make the most difficult decision of their lives, and consented to turning off life support for their daughter. Melissa passed away on September 28, 2004.

When the Galkas returned home from the hospital, they started getting signs from Melissa. "As soon as my wife and daughter got out of the car we could smell Melissa's perfume," Gary said. "And when we got into the house and were comforting each other the doorbell started ringing, but nobody was there. And that's never happened before."

Other strange electrical phenomena started happening for the Galkas. The TV would turn on and off or change channels by itself, and lights would flicker. Today Gary believes he was seeing his first signs of after-death communication, but he didn't recognize it at the time. He'd spent his career working as an engineer in electronics testing equipment, so the paranormal was very new to him.

Gary's other daughter saw an apparition of Melissa in the bathroom brushing her hair. His wife started having experiences she couldn't explain, like hearing Melissa call out "Mom." Gary would feel a phantom embrace and even a kiss on the cheek, though no one was there. The Galkas took a lot of comfort in this spirit contact.

After watching psychic Chris Fleming using a KII meter—a simple type of EMF meter that uses lights on a scale from green to yellow to red in order to measure the intensity of the electromagnetic field—on a ghost television show, he got curious and thought maybe a tool like this could validate his experiences and help him establish some much needed contact with the spirit of Melissa. Being an instrument engineer, Gary believed he could develop a better tool. His first meter would combine EMF and temperature readings, plus offer a recording feature so users could see the highs and lows during the recording period. He called this device the Mel-8704, after his daughter Melissa, born in '87, passed away in '04.

"The Mel meter was the fruition of all the passion I had for exploration and learning more about these things that I'd been exposed to, but I couldn't really put my finger on," Gary said.

Since the first version of the meter, Galka has been steadily adding to the device so it includes lights (like a KII meter), a flashlight feature, and room for expansion modules as he continues to build onto the device. It's a true all-in-one paranormal research tool.

I take a lot of comfort in knowing that the inventor of this device is so passionate about the subject, because for Gary Galka it's deeply personal.

When I use the Mel meter on an investigation, I'll reach for it as soon as activity seems to be going on in a certain area. If I'm getting strange feelings, I'll use the meter to try to validate whether there are temperature or EMF spikes going on. If so, I may be in a hot spot and I want to be sure my audio and cameras are recording . . . something paranormal could be close and I don't want to miss it.

AMPLIFIED E-POD: Electromagnetic energy isn't the only kind of energy floating around us. There's also electrostatic energy.

Electrostatic energy is easy to understand: try putting on wool socks and dragging your feet across dry carpet, then touch a metal doorknob. *Ouch!* You just created an electrostatic discharge. By rubbing your feet on the floor, you positively charged the atoms that then traveled through your body to the metal doorknob and sparked the discharge of energy, bringing everything back to neutral.

Electrostatic energy is all around us. The less moisture in the air, the more buildup can occur. Gary Galka helped develop the Amplified E-Pod to detect an electrostatic charge in the air around it. We've used this device on several episodes of *Ghost Adventures*, especially when the air is dry. We set this round canister down, extend the antenna from the top, turn it on, and leave it alone.

If there is a negative charge in the air, the green, blue, and red lights will dim and then go off as the negative charge gets stronger and moves closer to the E-Pod. If the conditions are positively charged, then the lights will be off at first, then begin to light up. The machine also makes a small alarm sound as the charge grows stronger—that is, closer to the antenna.

While walking through a paranormal hot spot, you can sometimes feel that the room is charged with energy. You may see us holding our arms out to watch the hair stand up. When that happens, we reach for the E-Pod to see if it also picks up the electrostatic energy that our bodies are feeling.

APPENDIX

PARANORMAL RESOURCES

Below is a list of Web sites and organizations that can help you learn more about the paranormal and the equipment we use to investigate.

NICK GROFF
You can find me on:
twitter: @NickGroff_
Tumblr: nickgroff-1.tumblr.com
YouTube: www.youtube.com/NickGroffVlogs
WhoSay: www.WhoSay.com/NickGroff

GHOST SHOP
www.ghostshop.com
The Web site of Bill Chappell and his various inventions including Ovilus X, EM pumps, EM Vortex, plus many others. Chappell is always coming up with something new to explore hauntings and ghostly phenomena.

PRO MEASURE
www.pro-measure.com

Pro Measure is the Web site for paranormal inventor Gary Galka, who's developed items like the Mel meter, E-Pods, and the SB7.

RHINE RESEARCH CENTER
www.rhine.org
For those looking to get more academic in their paranormal research. The Rhine Research Center was once Duke University's Parapsychology Laboratory. Founded in 1927 to study psychic phenomena, the organization spun off from the university in 2002 but maintains its mission to test and prove the existence of the afterlife. It has decades of data and experiments worth checking out.

AMERICAN INSTITUTE OF PARAPSYCHOLOGY
www.parapsychologylab.com
Founded by Dr. Andrew Nichols, this nonprofit organization studies anomalous human experiences involving the paranormal.

MARK AND DEBBY CONSTANTINO
www.spirits-speak.com
EVP specialists Mark and Debby Constantino have been working with *Ghost Adventures* for years. These two get amazing results with electronic voice phenomena. Their Web site features a gallery of their recordings and techniques.

ZAK BAGANS
www.zakbagans.com
The home page for Zak Bagans and information on all his endeavors.

AARON GOODWIN COLLECTIONS
www.agoodwincollections.com
Aaron Goodwin has a huge collection of his artwork, photography, and his Big Steppin line of clothing and products.

GHOSTVILLAGE.COM
www.ghostvillage.com
This site was founded by Jeff Belanger back in 1999 as a central location for all things ghostly. There are feature articles on the paranormal from believers, disbelievers, the religious, and the scientific, plus a collection of hundreds of ghost encounter experiences from all over the world.

DARKNESS RADIO
www.darknessradio.com
The home page of Dave Schrader and his *Darkness on the Edge of Town* radio show.

CHRIS FLEMING
www.unknownmagazine.com
The home page of psychic medium Chris Fleming. Chris joined us on the *Ghost Adventures* live episode and is a great resource for the psychic side of the paranormal.

PARANORMAL POP CULTURE
www.paranormalpopculture.com
The site of pop culture columnist Aaron Sagers. He examines all aspects of how the paranormal influences popular culture and vice versa.

COAST TO COAST AM

www.coasttocoastam.com

A nightly radio show that examines all aspects of the paranormal and the unusual. For decades this show has been among the first to examine what others have thought was impossible.

PARANORMAL PHENOMENA

paranormal.about.com

Paranormal guide Stephen Wagner has a huge stockpile of information on ghosts, hauntings, and many other aspects of the paranormal.

SKEPTIC MAGAZINE

www.skeptic.com

Founded by Dr. Michael Shermer, *Skeptic* magazine examines the other side of the paranormal debate: those who don't believe. Well worth reading—you may find your perspective broadened, but maybe you'll find some paranormal evidence that can hold up to the magazine's claims.

ABOUT THE AUTHORS

NICK GROFF has been fascinated with the paranormal since childhood—growing up in a haunted house will do that to you. Ever since his own near-death experience as a kid, Nick has been chasing ghosts for most of his life. As an adult, he's made a career out of investigating the supernatural. In addition to being one of the investigators and an executive producer for *Ghost Adventures*, Groff has worked as a director

Photo by Veronique Groff

and editor. After graduating from the University of Nevada with a BA in film, Groff worked his way through the production side of television, editing projects for networks like FOX, BET, MTV, and MTV-2. He was an actor and technician for the feature film *Primo* that screened at Sundance, and he cowrote, directed, produced, and edited the feature film *Malevolence* that screened at the prestigious CineVegas Film Festival.

In 2007, Groff had his big break when he cowrote, coproduced, codirected, coedited, and costarred in *Ghost Adventures:*

The Original Documentary, which aired on the SciFi Channel in 2007 and 2008. The film was a winner at the Los Angeles Film Festival and was nominated for "Best Feature Film" at the Eerie Horror Film Festival. The documentary led to the creation of *Ghost Adventures*, the television series that debuted on the Travel Channel in 2008 and is now in its sixth season; the show is now syndicated in eight countries. Groff is also the executive producer of the Travel Channel show *Vegas Stripped*.

Groff makes the rounds on the media circuit. He's been interviewed on the *Today* show, *Maury*, CNN, Howard Stern, many network affiliates, and numerous radio programs.

CONNECT ONLINE

www.WhoSay.com/NickGroff
twitter.com/NickGroff_
www.youtube.com/NickGroffVlogs
www.groffentertainment.com
nickgroff-1.tumblr.com

JEFF BELANGER is one of the most visible and prolific paranormal researchers today. He is a series writer and researcher for the *Ghost Adventures* series on the Travel Channel.

Belanger is the author of a dozen books on the paranormal (published in six languages), including *The World's Most Haunted Places*, *Our Haunted Lives*, and *Weird Massachusetts*. He's the founder of Ghostvillage.com, one of the Web's most popular paranormal destinations, and a noted lecturer on the subject of the unexplained, appearing at dozens of conferences, colleges, universities, and events each year.

Belanger is also the host of the weekly cable/Web talk show *30 Odd Minutes*. He has written for newspapers like the *Boston Globe* and has been a guest on hundreds of radio and television programs, including the History Channel, the Travel Channel, PBS, NECN, Living TV (UK), *Maury*, *CBS Sunday Morning*, CBS's *The Early Show*, network

Photo by Bleu Cotton Photography

affiliates, National Public Radio, BBC, Australian Radio Network, and *Coast to Coast AM*.

CONNECT ONLINE

www.jeffbelanger.com

www.ghostvillage.com

twitter.com/THEJeffBelanger